Pandemic Prevention: The Essential Guide to Avian Influenza.

Outbreak Control: Coordinated Response to Avian Flu.

By Nelson Smith.

Foreword by Kazuo Florence.

In the landscape of modern medicine and public health, few challenges are as urgent and complex as the threat of pandemics. "Pandemic Prevention: The Essential Guide to Avian Influenza," authored by the esteemed Nelson Smith, is a timely masterpiece that addresses this pressing issue with the gravity and diligence it deserves.

As a proponent of proactive health strategies, I, Kazuo Florence, have dedicated my life to understanding and combating infectious diseases. It is with great conviction that I endorse this seminal work, which stands as a pivotal resource for anyone seeking to comprehend and counteract the nuances of avian influenza.

Nelson Smith's profound insights are presented with clarity and precision, making this guide an indispensable tool for health professionals, policymakers, and laypersons alike. The book navigates through the historical precedents, current scenarios, and future projections of avian influenza with an authoritative voice that is both informative and accessible.

What sets this guide apart is its unwavering commitment to practicality. It does not merely present facts; it equips its readers with a strategic framework for pandemic prevention, offering actionable advice that can be implemented at individual, community, and global levels.

I urge you to delve into the pages of this guide, not just as a means of education but as a call to action. In a world where the next pandemic is not a question of 'if' but 'when,' "Pandemic Prevention: The Essential Guide to Avian Influenza" is more than a book—it is a beacon of hope and a blueprint for a healthier, safer future.

Kazuo Florence

Table of contents.

Introduction.

The Rising Threat of Avian Influenza.

Imagine a world where the flutter of a bird's wings carries more than just the promise of spring, but a silent threat that could unravel the tapestry of life as we know it. This is not a dystopian fantasy; it's the reality we face with the rising threat of avian influenza, a shadow looming over our interconnected world.

In the grand theatre of global health, avian influenza has emerged as a formidable antagonist, one that indiscriminately targets both wing and man. The narrative of bird flu is not merely a cautionary tale of an impending pandemic; it's a reflection of our intertwined existence with nature's delicate balance.

The stakes are monumental. The economic arteries that sustain our global village, the ecological harmony that whispers through our forests, and the social fabric that weaves our communities together—all stand at risk in the face of this viral adversary. The prevention of a bird flu pandemic transcends the act of averting a crisis; it is a testament to our resilience, our foresight, and our unwavering commitment to safeguarding the continuum of life.

Pandemic Prevention.
The Essential Guide to Avian Influenza"is not just a book; it is a conversation, a gathering of minds, and an urgent call to action. As we turn these pages, we embark on a journey through the complexities of a virus that knows no borders, a pathogen that has claimed the skies as its domain and the earth's creatures as its potential hosts.

The story of avian influenza is not a new one, but these chapters are being rewritten with alarming speed and intensity. The HPAI virus, with its notorious H5 strain, has become a master of disguise, mutating and outpacing our efforts to contain it. From the farmlands of Asia to the wilds of South America, it has left a trail of devastation, claiming the lives of millions of birds and jumping the species barrier with a ferocity that has caught humanity off guard.

But this is not a tale of despair. It's a narrative of resilience, science, and solidarity. It's about the farmers who watch over their flocks, the scientists who toil in their labs, and the policymakers who draft the blueprints for a safer tomorrow. It's about you and me, and how our choices—big and small—shape the health of our planet.

The Rising Threat of Avian Influenza.
Avian influenza, commonly known as bird flu, is an infectious viral disease of birds, often causing severe respiratory disease and, in some cases, affecting humans and other animals. The recent rise in avian influenza cases has raised global concerns due to its potential impact on wildlife, domestic animals, and human populations.

The Global Spread and Impact.
The High Pathogenic Avian Influenza (HPAI) virus has seen an unprecedented global spread, decimating wildlife populations and leading to the culling of over half a billion farmed birds.

The H5 strain and its variants have been particularly devastating, with millions of wild-bird deaths estimated in South America since 2023 alone[1]. The virus has also jumped species barriers, infecting at least 26 species of mammals, including cases in Denmark's mink farms and free-ranging bears in Canada.

Human Cases and Mortality.
While human cases have been relatively few, the mortality rate among those infected is alarmingly high, exceeding 50%. This high mortality rate underscores the potential threat to human health if the virus becomes more adept at human-to-human transmission.

Environmental and Ecological Concerns.
The virus's ability to spread to new regions and species has been linked to environmental changes and human activities. Climate change, in particular, may be altering bird migration patterns and habitats, facilitating the spread of the virus across continents and oceans.

Economic Consequences.
The economic impact of avian influenza is significant, affecting the poultry industry, trade, and livelihoods of farmers and workers. The loss of domestic poultry due to death or culling has financial repercussions that ripple through the food supply chain, leading to increased prices and food insecurity in affected regions.

Preventive Measures and Biosecurity.
Governments and health organisations have been implementing measures to prevent the spread of avian influenza. These include stringent biosecurity practices, monitoring of wild bird populations, and vaccination programs where feasible. Public awareness campaigns are also crucial in educating bird keepers and the general population about the signs of the disease and the steps to take to prevent its spread.

Research and Monitoring.
Ongoing research is essential to understand the virus's behaviour, transmission patterns, and potential mutations. Systematic monitoring, like

the expedition to Antarctica's Northern Weddell Sea, provides vital data to track the virus's spread and inform global response strategies.

The rising threat of avian influenza is a complex issue that requires a coordinated global response. It involves addressing the ecological, economic, and public health aspects of the disease. Continued vigilance, research, and international cooperation are key to mitigating the impact of this potentially devastating virus.

As we delve into the economic ripples, the ecological tremors, and the human cost of this avian adversary, we find glimmers of hope in the vigilance of communities, the advances in vaccine research, and the unwavering spirit of cooperation that defines our species at its best.

So, let us converse, let us learn, and let us prepare. The question of "Why Pandemic Prevention Matters" is not just the next topic of discussion—it's the cornerstone of our collective future, the answer to which lies in the unity of our actions and the wisdom of our choices. Welcome to the dialogue.

As I said earlier, avian influenza is not a distant threat lurking on the fringes of our world; it's a present and evolving danger that touches every aspect of our lives. The need for pandemic prevention is not just a matter of public health; it's a matter of global security, economic stability, and ecological balance.

Why Pandemic Prevention Matters.

In the grand theatre of global health, avian influenza has emerged as a formidable antagonist, one that indiscriminately targets both wing and man. The narrative of bird flu is not merely a cautionary tale of an impending pandemic; it's a reflection of our intertwined existence with nature's delicate balance.

The stakes are monumental.
The economic arteries that sustain our global village, the ecological harmony that whispers through our forests, and the social fabric that weaves our communities together—all stand at risk in the face of this viral adversary. The prevention of a bird flu pandemic transcends the act of averting a crisis; it is a testament to our resilience, our foresight, and our unwavering commitment to safeguarding the continuum of life.

The spectre of avian influenza casts a long shadow over our modern world. It's a virus that has shown us time and again its ability to disrupt and destroy, not just the lives of countless birds but the livelihoods of humans across the globe. The recent rise in cases and the virus's relentless spread are stark reminders of our vulnerability and the interconnectedness of life on Earth.

A Global Health Imperative.

Preventing a bird flu pandemic is not merely a cautionary measure; it's an imperative for global health. The high mortality rate among infected humans is a chilling warning of what could happen if the virus mutates to transmit more easily between people. We stand on the precipice of potential disaster, and pandemic prevention is the barrier holding back the tide.

Economic Resilience.

The economic impact of avian influenza is profound. The poultry industry is a cornerstone of global agriculture, providing sustenance and employment to millions. An outbreak can decimate this industry, leading to food shortages, price hikes, and economic turmoil. By preventing a pandemic, we protect not just our health but our economies as well.

Ecological Harmony.

Our ecosystems are delicate, and the loss of bird populations due to avian influenza can have cascading effects on biodiversity and ecological balance. Birds play crucial roles as pollinators, pest controllers, and seed dispersers. Protecting them from disease is essential to maintaining the harmony of our natural world.

Social Stability.
The fear and uncertainty that come with a pandemic can lead to social unrest and instability. Preventive measures help maintain public confidence and ensure that societies can function without the added strain of a health crisis.

Scientific Advancement.
Investing in pandemic prevention spurs scientific advancement. It drives research in virology, vaccine development, and disease modelling, pushing the boundaries of what we

know and can achieve in the realm of public health.

Moral Responsibility.

We have a moral responsibility to protect not just ourselves but all creatures with whom we share this planet. Preventing the spread of avian influenza is a testament to our commitment to life and the well-being of future generations.

As we pivot to our next discourse, we discuss the essence of avian influenza. It is a journey to demystify this pathogen, to strip it down to its core and understand its machinations. We will explore its origins, its capacity to wreak havoc across species, and the global tapestry of health systems that stand as our bulwark against its spread.

Join us as we define avian influenza not just as a disease, but as a global health concern that demands a unified front, a synergy of science, policy, and human will. It's a call to arms, to protect not just the human race, but every creature that calls this planet home.

In our forthcoming discussion, "We shall define Avian Influenza: A Global Health Concern," we will unravel the complexities of this disease, its impact on our world, and the collective measures we must embrace to ensure the narrative of avian influenza is one of triumph, not tragedy. Let's continue this vital conversation.

Chapter 1.

Avian Influenza 101.

Defining Avian Influenza: A Global Health Concern.

A Prelude to Caution.

Under the shadow of a flying menace, we are together and ready to take on avian influenza, a viral hazard that forces us to take action in order to avoid and safeguard.

Explanation of Avian Influenza.

Bird flu, often known as avian influenza, is a virus that mostly infects birds but may also infect people and other animals. Influenza type A viruses, which may infect domestic poultry as well as other bird and mammal species, are the source of this disease. They are found naturally in wild aquatic birds around the world. Humans are often not infected by avian flu viruses, however occasional human infections have happened.

A process known as reassortment may allow avian influenza to mix with human flu viruses, creating new viruses that may infect humans and spread quickly from person to person. This is why avian influenza is a cause for concern. This may cause the illness to spread globally and cause a pandemic.

Avian influenza strains are classified into two classes based on their pathogenicity, or ability to cause illness: low pathogenic avian influenza (LPAI) and high pathogenic avian influenza (HPAI). While HPAI causes severe disease and high mortality rates in birds, LPAI typically causes little symptoms that may go undetected.

The most prominent type, H5N1, has aroused concerns about its catastrophic impact on human health when transmitted from birds to humans. Although not widespread at the moment, the possibility of mutation makes human-to-human transmission a major global health concern.

A Global Health Concern.

As we go on to our next topic, "Avian Influenza: A Global Health Concern," we must recognize that the threat of avian influenza goes beyond its direct health consequences. It encompasses the readiness of our healthcare systems, economic resilience, and the long-term stability of our ecological networks. Understanding and battling avian influenza is more than just a scientific challenge; it is a moral responsibility to protect the health of all species on our planet.

This year, India reported its first mortality from H5N1 avian influenza.

Various ways to identify the virus.

What is the avian flu?

Also known as avian influenza.

It is a disease caused by avian influenza Type A viruses, which may be found naturally in wild birds across the world.

The virus may infect domestic poultry, and H5N1 infection has been reported in pigs, cats, and even tigers in Thai zoos.

Symptoms ranged from moderate to severe influenza-like illness.

H5N1 is a strain of influenza virus that causes avian influenza, a highly contagious and severe respiratory illness in birds. Human instances of H5N1 avian influenza are rare, although the illness is difficult to spread from person to person.

What sickness is known as H5N1?

It is a very severe strain of avian influenza (type A). It is harmful to birds, particularly waterfowl and poultry. The first human cases (18) were reported in Hong Kong in 1997, however the disease was quickly eradicated thanks to the city's outstanding public health system. It later resurfaced in Vietnam and Cambodia in 2003 and is still active. In 16 years, it has impacted around 800 people in 30 countries, with half of them dying. That is almost 50% case fatality rate (CFR), when most typical influenza is 0.1-0.2%.

The important component is the virus's place of attachment. H5N1 has developed to bind to target cells via alpha-sialic acid 3-6. In aquatic birds, this kind of cell is seen in the intestinal epithelium, indicating that the illness targets the enteric system. (The virus is discharged into open water bodies such as lakes and ponds, where fresh birds become infected, and so on. This form of attachment is prevalent in the lower respiratory tract in humans, thus those who have been infected have significant lung illness but do not cough or sneeze, which is required for the pandemic to spread.

The 1918 influenza pandemic remains the world's worst epidemic in a single year. Its CFR was roughly 2.5 percent. The prevalence of H5N1 is 20 times higher.

What is the definition of H5N1 avian influenza?

This year, India has documented its first fatality from H5N1 avian influenza.

So, what exactly is avian flu?

Avian influenza is another name for this virus.

It is a disease caused by avian influenza Type A viruses, which may be found naturally in wild birds across the world.

The virus may infect domestic poultry, and H5N1 infection has been observed in Thai zoos in pigs, cats, and even tigers.

The symptoms ranged from moderate to severe flu-like sickness.

Classification:

Avian Influenza type A viruses are identified by two proteins on their surfaces: Hemagglutinin (HA) and Neuraminidase (NA).

There are around 18 HA and 11 NA subtypes. Several combinations of these two proteins are conceivable, including H5N1, H7N2, H9N6, and H17N10.

Spread:

There have been reports of avian and swine influenza infections in humans.

The infection is deadly as it has a high mortality rate of about 60%.

The most common route of virus transmission is direct contact. They can also be affected if they come in contact with contaminated surfaces or air near the infected poultry.

H5N1 is a type of influenza virus that causes a highly infectious, severe respiratory disease in birds called avian influenza (or "bird flu"). Human cases of H5N1 avian influenza occur occasionally, but it is difficult to transmit the infection from person to person

What illness is sometimes referred to as H5N1?

It is a particularly severe form of avian influenza (type A). For birds, especially water birds and poultry, it's lethal. The first human cases (18) emerged in Hong Kong in 1997, but due to the excellent public health system there, it was stamped out. It then re-emerged in VietNam and Cambodia in 2003 and is still going. In 16 years it has affected around 800 humans in around 30 countries, of whom half have died. That's about 50% case fatality rate (CFR), whereas most normal influenza is 0.1 - 0.2%

The important component is the virus's place of attachment. H5N1 has developed to bind to target cells via alpha-sialic acid 3-6. In aquatic birds, this kind of cell is seen in the intestinal epithelium, indicating that the illness targets the enteric system. (The virus is discharged into open water bodies such as lakes and ponds, where fresh birds become infected, and so on. This form of attachment is prevalent in the lower respiratory tract in humans, thus those who have been infected have significant lung illness but do not cough or sneeze, which is required for the pandemic to spread.

The 1918 influenza pandemic remains the world's worst epidemic in a single year. Its CFR was roughly 2.5 percent. H5N1 is twenty times more prevalent.

H5N1Avian influenza, also known as Asian highly pathogenic avian influenza, is caused by the (HPAI) A(H5N1) virus and mostly affects birds. It is very infectious among them. HPAI Asian H5N1 is very harmful to poultry. The virus was discovered in 1996 in geese in China.

Asian H5N1 was initially identified in humans in 1997 during a poultry outbreak in Hong Kong, and it has subsequently been found in poultry and wild birds in over 50 countries across Africa, Asia, Europe, and the Middle East.

Most human infections with Asian H5N1 viruses in other countries have resulted from prolonged and intimate contact with infected ill or dead birds.

Although human infections with this virus are uncommon, around 60% of instances resulted in death.

The bulk of human infections with Asian HPAI H5N1 have been among youngsters and individuals under the age of forty. Mortality has been higher among those aged 10 to 19 years old and young adults. The majority of Asian human HPAI H5N1 cases arrived for treatment at a later stage of their illness and were admitted to the hospital due to serious respiratory complications. However, several clinically mild instances have been observed, particularly among youngsters.

Asian HPAI H5N1 viruses have infected humans' respiratory tracts, resulting in serious sickness (e.g., pneumonia and respiratory failure) and death in certain cases.

About 55% of those who contract the H5N1 bird flu die from it (medicalnet.com).

NASA has discovered that H5N1 is spread via saliva from infected birds.

What exactly is H1N1 influenza?

The influenza A virus has undergone a mutation known as H1N1. Without getting too technical, the "H" and "N" represent antigens on the virus that designate its subtype. Flu viruses continually change, therefore there are several subtypes up to and including H7N9.

Some refer to H1N1 as "swine flu" because it has a reservoir in pigs. However, H1N1 has been present for almost a century. It was responsible for the 1918 influenza pandemic, which killed between 50 and 100 million people. It appears to be less deadly now, most likely because vaccination efforts have made more people immune to it.

H1N1 is especially hazardous because of how the body reacts to the flu virus.

Although you may be immune to H1N1 due to vaccination or infection, this is not the end of the tale. New strains of influenza A are equally deadly. The H5N1 type, sometimes known as the "bird flu," generates the same symptoms as the 1918 pandemic. It is extremely pathogenic and might cause a similar-sized pandemic. It is similar to the H1N1 version, but the mutations make it far worse.

The Biology and Transmission of the Bird Flu Virus.

As we continue our trip through the complex world of avian influenza, let us consider our prior conversations. We discovered the disease's growing threat, its worldwide impact, and the need for pandemic preparedness. Now, we will look further into the biology of this cryptic virus and the processes that drive its infamous proliferation.

Avian influenza, sometimes known as bird flu, is caused by influenza A viruses that are indigenous to diverse bird species. These viruses are segmented RNA viruses, which means that their genetic material is separated into many parts, allowing them to reassort and change quickly. This feature is what makes them so hazardous; it allows the virus to rapidly adapt to various hosts and situations.

Wild ducks serve as a natural reservoir for many viruses, as they may carry the infection without exhibiting symptoms. However, when these viruses infect domestic chickens, they may become extremely pathogenic, causing severe sickness and significant fatality rates. The virus spreads more easily among birds due to their migratory tendencies, which might bring the infection to new locations and populations.

Human infections with avian influenza are uncommon, although they can develop following direct or indirect contact with infected animals. The danger is that if the virus develops the capacity to travel readily from person to person, it might trigger a pandemic with disastrous effects.

Transmission Dynamics for Avian Influenza.
Understanding the transmission mechanisms of avian influenza is critical to curbing its spread. The virus can spread by direct contact with infected birds, their droppings, or contaminated surfaces. Airborne transmission is also conceivable, particularly in confined environments such as chicken farms.

The virus's capacity to infect various species, including humans, pigs, and other animals, raises the possibility of reassortment with human flu viruses. This might create a new strain capable of sparking a human pandemic.

Vaccination of poultry, culling of sick flocks, and rigorous biosecurity measures are critical tactics for controlling avian influenza transmission. Public health measures, such as surveillance and prompt reaction to outbreaks, are also crucial in preventing human infections and limiting the virus's spread.

Next Topic for Discussion: Historical Outbreaks.

Looking ahead, our next subject of discussion will be previous outbreaks of avian influenza. We will look at previous events, such as the H5N1 pandemic in Hong Kong in 1997 and the large H7N9 outbreak in China in 2013. These incidents teach important insights about the virus's behaviour, the efficacy of response tactics, and the significance of worldwide collaboration in handling such threats.

By studying past outbreaks, we may gain a better understanding of the problems we confront and the efforts we must take to prevent future pandemics. Join us as we dig into history to arm ourselves with information and prepare for future fights in our continuing combat against avian influenza.

Chapter 2:

Historical Outbreaks.

A Timeline of Avian Influenza Outbreaks.

In our previous discussions, we delved into various topics ranging from technological advancements to historical events, always aiming to provide insightful and accurate information. We've explored subjects with depth and context, ensuring a comprehensive understanding of each topic.

Historical Outbreaks of Avian Influenza.
Avian influenza, also known as bird flu, has a long and complex history that spans over a century. The disease is caused by influenza viruses that occur naturally among wild aquatic birds worldwide and can infect domestic poultry and other bird and animal species. Avian flu

viruses do not normally infect humans. However, sporadic human infections with avian flu viruses have occurred. Here is a timeline of significant avian influenza outbreaks:

- **1880s-1950s**:

-**1878**: The first well-documented case of highly pathogenic avian influenza (HPAI) occurred in Italy. It was later identified as HPAI H7N7.

-**1955**: The avian influenza virus was first identified as a Type A influenza virus.

- **1960s-1990s**:

- **1961**: An outbreak of HPAI H5N2 occurred in Scotland.

- **1983**: A significant outbreak in the United States led to the culling of 17 million birds.

- **1996**: The H5N1 strain emerged in China, leading to the first recorded transmission to humans in 1997.

- **2000s**:
- **2003**: HPAI H7N7 outbreaks in the Netherlands caused one human fatality.
- **2004-2005**: The H5N1 virus spread across Asia, Europe, and Africa, resulting in the culling of over 150 million birds.
- **2008**: HPAI H7N3 outbreak in Canada.

- **2010s**:
- **2013**: China reported human infections with a new avian influenza A (H7N9) virus.
- **2014-2015**: Outbreaks of HPAI H5 viruses, including H5N2, H5N8, and H5N6, were reported in Asia, Europe, and North America.
- **2016**: An outbreak of HPAI H7N8 occurred in the United States.

2020s:
- **2020**: The emergence of HPAI H5N1 with genes from wild birds was first identified in Europe and spread across continents[1].
- **2021**: Reports of HPAI H5N8 in seals in the United Kingdom and other countries. Laos

reported its first human infection with HPAI H5N6.

The timeline of avian influenza outbreaks shows the recurring nature of the disease and the constant evolution of the virus. Each outbreak has provided valuable lessons in disease management and prevention. The global response has involved cooperation between countries, the sharing of information, and the implementation of comprehensive control measures. Organisations like the World Health Organization (WHO) and the Food and Agriculture Organization (FAO) play pivotal roles in coordinating these efforts.

Preventing future outbreaks requires a multifaceted approach, including improving biosecurity in poultry farms, developing and distributing effective vaccines, and enhancing surveillance systems to detect and respond to outbreaks promptly. Public education campaigns are also crucial to inform people about the risks and measures they can take to protect themselves and their livestock.

Research into avian influenza continues to be vital. Understanding the virus's behaviour, transmission patterns, and genetic changes will be key to developing new strategies to prevent and control outbreaks. The aim is not only to protect animal health but also to safeguard human health and the global economy from the impacts of this formidable disease.

Avian influenza, commonly known as bird flu, has a storied history that traces back to the late 19th century. The earliest recorded instance of this disease was in 1878 in Italy, where it was initially referred to as "fowl plague" due to its high mortality rate among poultry. It wasn't until 1955 that the causative agent was identified as a Type A influenza virus. This discovery marked a significant milestone in understanding and combating the disease.

As the 20th century progressed, the world witnessed several outbreaks of varying magnitudes. In 1983, for example, an outbreak in Pennsylvania, USA, resulted in the culling of 17 million birds to contain the virus. The economic impact was substantial, highlighting the need for better control and prevention strategies.

The turn of the millennium saw the emergence of the highly pathogenic H5N1 strain, which first appeared in China in 1996. This strain proved to be particularly virulent, with the ability to infect humans and cause severe respiratory illness. The subsequent outbreaks across Asia in the early 2000s led to the culling of hundreds of millions of birds and resulted in significant human fatalities.

Efforts to manage avian influenza have evolved over the years, with a focus on surveillance, biosecurity measures, and the development of vaccines. Despite these efforts, the virus continues to pose a threat due to its capacity for mutation and species jumping.

In recent years, we've seen outbreaks of various strains like H7N9 and H5N8, which have affected not only birds but also other animals and humans. The outbreak of H5N8 in 2020, for example, spread across Europe and Asia, affecting wild birds, poultry, and even mammals like seals and foxes. This underscores the virus's ability to adapt and spread across different species.

The global response to avian influenza involves cooperation between countries, the sharing of information, and the implementation of comprehensive control measures. Organisations like the World Health Organization (WHO) and the Food and Agriculture Organization (FAO) play pivotal roles in coordinating these efforts.

Preventing future outbreaks requires a multifaceted approach. This includes improving biosecurity in poultry farms, developing and distributing effective vaccines, and enhancing surveillance systems to detect and respond to outbreaks promptly. Public education campaigns are also crucial to inform people about the risks and measures they can take to protect themselves and their livestock.

As we look to the future, research into avian influenza will continue to be vital. Understanding the virus's behaviour, transmission patterns, and genetic changes will be key to developing new strategies to prevent and control outbreaks. The aim is not only to protect animal health but also to safeguard human health and the global economy from the impacts of this formidable disease.

In conclusion, the history of avian influenza is a testament to the ongoing battle between humanity and viral diseases. From the first outbreak in Italy to the global spread of H5N1 and beyond, each incident has provided valuable lessons. These lessons shape our current strategies and our resolve to prevent future pandemics, ensuring that we are better prepared for whatever challenges avian influenza may present in the years to come.

Our next topic, **"Learning from Past Pandemics**," will focus on how historical pandemics have shaped public health responses and preparedness. We'll examine the lessons learned and how they inform current strategies to combat infectious diseases.

Learning from Past Pandemic.

In our last exchange, we discussed the historical outbreaks of avian influenza, examining the timeline of significant events and the evolution of the virus. We emphasised the importance of global cooperation and vigilance to prevent future pandemics, and the ongoing efforts to safeguard both animal and human health.

Learning from Past Bird Flu Pandemics.

The history of bird flu pandemics is a chronicle of humanity's ongoing struggle with viral diseases that jump from animals to humans. The **H5N1 avian influenza** outbreak in 1996 was a wake-up call, as it crossed species barriers and infected humans, leading to severe respiratory illnesses and deaths. This event underscored the need for better surveillance and control measures in poultry farming, which were implemented in many countries.

However, despite these efforts, the virus persisted and evolved, leading to further outbreaks. The **H7N9 virus** in 2013 in China, for example, resulted in a high mortality rate among humans, prompting a massive culling of poultry and the development of new vaccines. These responses were crucial in containing the outbreaks, but they also highlighted the economic and social costs of such pandemics.

The **ongoing H5N8 outbreak** has been particularly alarming, as it has affected not only birds but also mammals, indicating the virus's ability to adapt and spread across different species. This has raised concerns about the potential for a human pandemic and the urgent need for a coordinated global response.

Learning from these past pandemics, it is clear that we must take immediate and decisive action to prevent future outbreaks. This includes investing in research to understand the virus's behaviour and transmission patterns, enhancing biosecurity measures in poultry farms, and ensuring the rapid distribution of vaccines. Public education is also vital to inform people about the risks and the steps they can take to protect themselves and their animals.

Moreover, we must address the environmental factors that contribute to the emergence and spread of such viruses, such as habitat destruction and the wildlife trade. Only by tackling these root causes can we hope to prevent the spillover of viruses from animals to humans.

Avian influenza, often known as bird flu, has been a subject of concern since the 18th century. The disease, caused by influenza viruses that naturally occur in wild birds, has led to numerous outbreaks affecting both animal and human health. Here, we explore case studies and analyses of avian influenza from its earliest recorded instances to the present day.

18th and 19th Centuries.

The first documented case of avian influenza occurred in 1878 in Italy, where it was referred to as "fowl plague." This outbreak was characterised by high mortality rates among poultry, but it would take nearly a century before the causative agent was identified as an influenza virus.

20th Century.

The 20th century saw several significant outbreaks of avian influenza. In 1955, the virus was classified as a Type A influenza virus, leading to a better understanding of the disease and its management. The latter half of the century experienced outbreaks of various strains, including H5N2 in Scotland in 1961 and a devastating HPAI H5N2 outbreak in the United States in 1983, which resulted in the culling of 17 million birds.

21st Century.

The emergence of the highly pathogenic H5N1 strain in 1996 in China marked a turning point in the history of avian influenza. This strain demonstrated the potential for avian viruses to infect humans, causing severe respiratory illnesses and fatalities. The early 2000s saw the spread of H5N1 across Asia, Europe, and Africa, leading to the culling of over 150 million birds and significant human deaths.

Recent years have continued to see outbreaks of various strains, such as H7N9 in China in 2013 and the widespread H5N8 outbreak in 2020, which affected birds and mammals across Europe and Asia. These outbreaks have highlighted the need for ongoing surveillance, research, and global cooperation to manage the disease effectively.

Case Studies and Analyses.
Surveillance studies have established that aquatic birds are the natural reservoirs of influenza A viruses, which can occasionally spread to domestic avian species and mammals, including humans. Research has focused on understanding the ecology of influenza in wild birds and the factors that contribute to the zoonotic spread of the virus. One of the unresolved issues is whether all H5 and H7 viruses have high pandemic potential and whether the highly pathogenic H5N1 virus is now being perpetuated in wild birds.

Analyses of past outbreaks have led to the development of mechanistic models to study avian influenza transmission and control strategies. These models help estimate parameters for low pathogenicity and highly pathogenic avian influenza transmission, providing insights into the efficacy of various control measures.

Prevention and Control.
The case studies and analyses of avian influenza have informed prevention and control strategies. These include improving biosecurity measures in poultry farms, developing vaccines, and enhancing surveillance systems. Public education campaigns play a crucial role in informing people about the risks and preventive measures.

The history of avian influenza is marked by recurring outbreaks and the continuous evolution of the virus. Case studies and analyses have been instrumental in shaping our understanding and response to the disease. As we move forward, it is essential to maintain vigilance and adapt our strategies to prevent and control future outbreaks, ensuring the safety of both animal and human populations.

Next Topic - Symptoms Identification:**
Identifying symptoms is the first step in combating any disease. Our next discussion will unravel the intricacies of symptom identification, equipping readers with knowledge that could be life-saving and emphasising the importance of early detection in disease management. Stay tuned to learn how to become your health advocate in an ever-changing world of medical challenges.

As we look to the future, the lessons from past bird flu pandemics must guide our actions. We need to build stronger health systems, develop more effective vaccines, and foster international cooperation to combat these threats. The stakes are high, and the time to act is now.

Chapter 3.

Identifying Symptoms.

Early Detection: Symptoms in Birds and Humans.

The Enigma of Avian Influenza:
A Tale of Symptoms in Feathers and Flesh.
Avian influenza, a viral infection that primarily affects birds, has occasionally crossed the species barrier to infect humans, leading to serious health concerns. The symptoms of this disease can be as varied as the species it infects, painting a complex picture of its impact on health.

In Birds.
The symptoms in birds can range from mild to severe, often depending on the strain of the virus. Mild symptoms may include ruffled feathers and a slight reduction in egg production.

However, more severe symptoms can lead to sudden death. These include:
- Swelling of the head, eyelids, comb, wattles, and hocks
- Purple discoloration of the wattles, combs, and legs
- Nasal discharge, coughing, and sneezing
- Lack of coordination
- Diarrhoea

Highly pathogenic strains, like H5N1, can spread rapidly through poultry flocks, causing disease that affects multiple internal organs and has a mortality rate that can reach 100% within 48 hours.

In Humans.

Human infections with avian influenza are rare, but when they occur, the symptoms can be severe and life-threatening. Early symptoms often mimic those of conventional influenza, including:
- Fever
- Cough
- Sore throat
- Muscle aches

As the infection progresses, individuals may experience more severe respiratory symptoms, including pneumonia and Acute Respiratory Distress Syndrome (ARDS). Other symptoms might include:
- Conjunctivitis
- Abdominal pain
- Vomiting
- Diarrhoea

In some cases, the infection can lead to complications such as sepsis, organ failure, and death. The severity of the disease in humans can be influenced by the strain of the virus and the individual's underlying health conditions.

Prevention and Control:

Preventing avian influenza involves biosecurity measures such as isolating poultry from wild birds, vaccination of domestic birds, and proper cooking of poultry products. For humans, avoiding contact with infected birds, using protective gear when handling poultry, and adhering to travel advisories are key preventive strategies.

Understanding the symptoms of avian influenza in both birds and humans is crucial for early detection and response. While the disease poses a significant threat to both animal and human health, ongoing research and surveillance are essential to mitigate its impact.

Risk Factors for Human Avian Influenza: Feathered Threats and Silent Transmission.

Avian influenza, colloquially known as bird flu, dances on the delicate edge between feathered flocks and human vulnerability. Let us unravel the risk factors that weave this intricate tapestry of disease transmission.

In Birds:
1. **Direct Contact with Infected Poultry**: The primary risk factor for avian influenza in humans stems from close encounters with live or dead infected birds. Handling poultry, especially during culling or de-feathering, poses a significant threat.
2. **Wild Swan Exposure**: A few cases have arisen from contact with infected wild swans. These majestic creatures, carriers of the virus, harbour danger beneath their graceful wings.

In Humans:

1. **Consumption of Uncooked Poultry**: Consuming undercooked poultry products can lead to human infections. Beware the siren call of raw delicacies; they may harbour more than flavour.

2. **Spillover from Birds to Humans**: Proximity to infected birds, whether in live bird markets or domestic settings, increases the risk. The virus tiptoes across species boundaries, seeking its next host.

Risk Levels:

- **Level 0 (Baseline):** Avian influenza circulates within normal bounds among birds.
- **Level 1:** Altered epidemiological dynamics or increased prevalence in bird populations.
- **Level 2:** Spillover into mammals detected.
- **Level 3:** Viral genomic changes favouring mammalian infection.

- **Level 4**: Sustained transmission in non-human mammals or human detection with specific mutations.
- **Level 5:** Human-to-human transmission—our ultimate nightmare.

Currently, the UK assesses the risk at **Level 3**, where viral whispers hint at adaptation. Vigilance remains our armour.

How can we improve early detection of bird flu outbreaks?

Improving early detection of bird flu outbreaks is crucial for preventing their spread and minimising impact on both animal and human health. Here are some strategies that can enhance early detection:

1. **Enhanced Surveillance**: Increasing surveillance efforts in wild bird populations and poultry farms can help detect outbreaks before they spread. This includes regular sampling and testing of birds.

2. **Rapid Diagnostic Testing**: Utilising rapid diagnostic tests like real-time polymerase chain reaction (RT-PCR) can provide quick and accurate detection of avian influenza viruses.

3. **Genomic Sequencing**: Implementing genomic sequencing can identify and track different strains of avian influenza, providing insights into their evolution and spread.

4. **Wastewater Surveillance**: Monitoring wastewater from poultry farms can detect viral shedding even before clinical signs are observed in birds.

5. **Biosecurity Measures**: Strengthening biosecurity practices on farms, such as controlling access to poultry areas and

disinfecting equipment, can prevent the introduction and spread of the virus.

6. **Public Health Guidelines**: Adhering to public health guidelines during outbreaks, including culling infected flocks and enforcing farm biosecurity, is essential for containment.

7. **Education and Training**: Educating farmers, veterinarians, and the public about avian influenza and its symptoms can lead to quicker reporting and response to potential outbreaks[1].

8. **International Cooperation**: Sharing information and resources between countries can lead to better preparedness and response to avian influenza outbreaks globally.
By implementing these measures, we can improve our ability to detect avian influenza outbreaks early and respond effectively to protect both animal and human health.

Next Topic - The Diagnostic Process for Avian Influenza:
Join us as we delve into the diagnostic labyrinth of avian influenza, where every clue unravels part of the viral mystery. Our next discussion promises to illuminate the path from suspicion to confirmation, arming you with knowledge to navigate the complexities of disease detection.

The Diagnostic Process for Avian Influenza.

The Diagnostic Odyssey: Unravelling Avian Influenza in Birds and Humans.

Avian influenza, a viral disease that primarily affects birds, has the potential to infect humans, posing significant health risks. The diagnostic process for avian influenza is a meticulous journey, one that requires precision and expertise. Let's explore this process, categorised under birds and humans, and suggest queries for a comprehensive understanding.

In Birds:

The diagnosis of avian influenza in birds involves several steps:

1. **Clinical Observation**: The first line of detection often comes from observing clinical signs in birds, such as respiratory distress, diarrhoea, and sudden death.

2. **Sample Collection**: Samples such as swabs from the throat or cloaca, and tissue samples from deceased birds, are collected for testing.

3. **Molecular Testing**: Tests like real-time RT-PCR are used to detect the viral genome in samples, providing a quick and accurate diagnosis.

4. **Virus Isolation**: In some cases, the virus is isolated in embryonated chicken eggs or cell cultures for further analysis.

5. **Serological Testing**: Tests like ELISA or hemagglutination inhibition (HI) assay detect antibodies against the virus, indicating exposure.

6. **Pathotyping**: To determine the pathogenicity of the virus, sequences of the hemagglutinin (HA) gene are analysed.

In Humans:

The diagnostic process for avian influenza in humans includes:

1. **Clinical Criteria**: Initial assessment based on symptoms such as fever, cough, and shortness of breath, especially in individuals with a history of exposure to infected birds.

2. **Sample Collection**: Swabs from the upper respiratory tract (nose or throat) are collected, preferably during the early stages of illness.

3. **Laboratory Testing**: Molecular tests like RT-PCR are performed to detect the presence of avian influenza viruses.

4. **Subtyping**: If influenza A is detected, further testing is done to subtype the virus and confirm if it is of avian origin.

5. **Virus Isolation**: Similar to birds, virus isolation can be performed for human samples.

6. **Serological Testing**: Blood tests can identify antibodies against avian influenza, indicating past infection.

Navigating the Symptoms and Science of Avian Influenza Diagnosis.

Avian influenza, a viral infection that has captured global attention, poses significant risks to both birds and humans. Understanding the symptoms that warrant testing and the diagnostic tools at our disposal is crucial for controlling its spread. This article delves into the symptoms indicative of avian influenza, the use of RT-PCR in diagnosis, the role of virus isolation, and the contribution of serological tests in both birds and humans.

Symptoms Prompting Testing for Avian Influenza:

In **birds**, avian influenza symptoms can range from mild to severe. Mild cases may present with ruffled feathers and reduced egg production, while severe cases can lead to respiratory distress, swelling of the head, and sudden death.

In **humans**, symptoms often resemble those of seasonal flu, including fever, cough, and sore throat, but can progress to severe respiratory issues like pneumonia. Particularly, individuals exposed to infected birds or contaminated environments should be tested.

RT-PCR in Avian Influenza Diagnosis:

Real-time Reverse Transcription Polymerase Chain Reaction (RT-PCR) is a cornerstone in diagnosing avian influenza in both **birds** and **humans**. This technique amplifies the virus's genetic material to detectable levels, providing a rapid and accurate diagnosis. In **birds**, it helps confirm the presence of the virus in flocks, while in **humans**, it is used to identify the specific strain of influenza virus, crucial for treatment and epidemiological tracking.

The Role of Virus Isolation:

Virus isolation involves growing the virus from samples in a controlled environment, such as in embryonated eggs or cell cultures. In **birds**, this method confirms the diagnosis and allows for further characterization of the virus.

In **humans**, virus isolation can provide definitive proof of infection and is essential for vaccine development and understanding the virus's behaviour.

Contribution of Serological Tests:

Serological tests detect antibodies against the virus, indicating exposure. In **birds**, these tests can identify past infections and the level of immunity in a flock.

In **humans**, serological tests are used to confirm previous infections, especially in cases where the virus is no longer present but has triggered an immune response.

The detection and diagnosis of avian influenza require a multifaceted approach, combining clinical observation with sophisticated laboratory techniques. By understanding the symptoms and utilising RT-PCR, virus isolation, and serological tests, we can enhance our ability to detect and respond to avian influenza outbreaks, safeguarding both animal and human health.

Step into the vanguard of defence against avian influenza with our next enlightening topic: "Prevention Strategies." Uncover the pivotal actions that can fortify birds and humans against this viral adversary, ensuring a future where health soars above disease. Prepare to be empowered with knowledge that can turn the tide in our perpetual quest for safety and well-being. Join us to learn, engage, and protect.

Chapter 4

Prevention Strategies.

Vaccination and Its Role in Prevention.

The Unseen Shield: Vaccinations Role in Thwarting Avian Influenza.

In the spring of 2024, a Texas farm worker's life changed dramatically. After exposure to dairy cattle presumed infected with H5N1, he became the first person to contract the virus from a cow. This incident not only highlighted the virus's unpredictable nature but also underscored the urgent need for effective vaccines.

Vaccination has played a critical role in preventing and controlling the spread of diseases, including Avian Influenza. Avian Influenza, also known as bird flu, is a highly contagious viral disease that affects birds, and in some cases, it can also infect humans. Vaccination is a crucial tool in combating Avian Influenza as it helps to reduce the spread of the virus among bird populations and lowers the risk of transmission to humans.

Vaccines for Avian Influenza are designed to stimulate the immune system of birds, thereby preparing them to effectively combat the virus if they are exposed to it. This can significantly reduce the severity of the disease and decrease the likelihood of mortality among the bird population. Additionally, by reducing the viral load in birds, vaccination can help to minimise the risk of transmission to humans, thus playing a crucial role in preventing potential pandemics.

Furthermore, vaccination against Avian Influenza is an essential component of broader control and prevention strategies. When used in conjunction with other measures such as biosecurity protocols, surveillance, and monitoring, vaccination can contribute to the overall reduction of disease prevalence and the containment of outbreaks. This multi-faceted approach is particularly important in regions where Avian Influenza is endemic or where there is a high risk of transmission to humans.

In the context of public health, the use of vaccines for Avian Influenza serves as a crucial line of defence against the potential emergence of new viral strains with pandemic potential. By reducing the prevalence of the virus in bird populations, vaccination can help minimise the opportunities for the virus to mutate and potentially pose a threat to human health. This is especially pertinent given the potential for Avian Influenza viruses to reassort and acquire genetic characteristics that make them more transmissible and virulent in humans.

In short, vaccination plays a pivotal role in the prevention and control of Avian Influenza. By bolstering the immune response of birds and limiting viral transmission, vaccines are an indispensable tool in mitigating the impact of this disease on both animal and human health. As part of comprehensive disease management strategies, vaccination is essential for minimising the risks associated with Avian Influenza and safeguarding public health.

Vaccinations Role in Birds:

Vaccination in birds, particularly poultry, is a complex issue. While vaccines can reduce mortality, there's a concern that vaccinated birds might still transmit the disease. In the UK, vaccination of birds is generally not permitted, except for zoo birds under strict conditions. The development of DIVA (Differentiating Infected from Vaccinated Animals) vaccines is a priority, aiming to allow differentiation between infected and vaccinated birds, which could revolutionise outbreak management.

Vaccinations Role in Humans:
For humans, vaccination remains the most effective strategy for avian influenza prevention and control, despite varying vaccine efficacy across strains[9]. Seasonal influenza vaccination is recommended for those occupationally exposed to potentially infected animals, reducing the likelihood of co-infection with zoonotic and seasonal influenza viruses.

Access to Vaccines:

Access to avian influenza vaccines varies by region and need. In the UK, zoo birds can be vaccinated under strict conditions, but this is not the case for poultry or other captive birds. For humans, while there is no specific avian influenza vaccine widely available yet, the U.S. Government is developing A (H5N1) bird flu vaccines in case they are needed. It's essential to consult local health authorities or the World Health Organization for the latest information on vaccine availability and recommendations.

The story of the Texas farm worker is a stark reminder of the ever-present threat of avian influenza and the indispensable role of vaccination in preventing its spread. As we continue to witness the virus's ability to jump species, the development and accessibility of effective vaccines for both birds and humans become paramount in our defence against this formidable viral foe.

Biosecurity Measures to Protect Poultry and Humans.

Biosecurity measures are essential for protecting both poultry and humans from the potential risks associated with infectious diseases. These measures aim to prevent the spread of diseases, minimise the impact of outbreaks, and safeguard the health and well-being of both poultry and humans.

One of the fundamental aspects of biosecurity is controlling the movement of people, animals, and equipment onto and within poultry premises. This helps in limiting the introduction and potential spread of diseases. All individuals entering a poultry facility should adhere to strict biosecurity protocols such as wearing appropriate protective clothing, disinfecting footwear, and following designated pathways to minimise the risk of disease transmission.

Furthermore, maintaining strict hygienic practices within the poultry farm is crucial. Regular cleaning and disinfection of facilities, equipment, and vehicles can significantly reduce the risk of disease transmission. Proper waste management and disposal also play a vital role in preventing the spread of pathogens. Implementing these measures effectively requires clear guidelines and regular training of personnel to ensure compliance.

In addition to physical biosecurity measures, it is imperative to manage the health of the poultry flock through vaccination, regular health monitoring, and prompt disease diagnosis. Vaccination against prevalent diseases can substantially reduce the risk of outbreaks and limit the impact of infections. Regular health monitoring allows for early detection of any potential issues, enabling swift action to contain and manage the situation. Prompt disease diagnosis, often through laboratory testing, is vital in implementing targeted control measures.

Strict controls on the movement of live birds, poultry products, and by-products are also necessary to prevent the spread of diseases between different locations. This includes regulating the transportation of poultry, eggs, and related materials to minimise the risk of introducing infections to new areas. Additionally, monitoring and controlling the movement of wild birds, pests, and vermin around poultry facilities can help mitigate the risk of disease transmission.

Education and awareness play a critical role in ensuring the successful implementation of biosecurity measures. Farmers, workers, and all individuals involved in the poultry industry should be knowledgeable about the importance of biosecurity and be trained in the necessary protocols. This includes understanding disease risks, recognizing clinical signs of illness, and knowing how to respond effectively in the event of a potential disease threat.

Furthermore, collaboration and communication among poultry producers, veterinary professionals, industry stakeholders, and relevant governmental agencies are essential for sharing information, coordinating responses to potential outbreaks, and establishing unified biosecurity standards.

It is important to recognize that biosecurity measures not only protect poultry but also have significant implications for public health. Many infectious diseases affecting poultry can also pose a risk to human health. By implementing robust biosecurity measures, the potential transmission of zoonotic diseases can be minimised, thus safeguarding the health of individuals involved in the poultry industry and the broader population.

Effective biosecurity measures are fundamental for protecting both poultry and humans from the risks associated with infectious diseases. These measures encompass a wide range of strategies, including controlling movement into and within poultry premises, maintaining strict hygiene practices, managing flock health, regulating the movement of live birds and poultry products, and promoting education and collaboration within the industry. By prioritising biosecurity, we can safeguard the welfare of poultry, protect public health, and ensure the sustainability of the poultry industry.

Chapter 5.

Containment and Control.

Responding to an Outbreak: Containment Protocols.

In light of the recent prevalence of avian influenza, it is imperative to delve into the strategies and frameworks laid down for containing and mitigating the outbreak. The impact of bird flu has precipitated a cascade of complexities that demand critical attention and a concerted effort to curtail its spread.

First and foremost, the containment protocols for avian influenza are multifaceted, encompassing various domains of public health, veterinary medicine, and epidemiology. The amalgamation of these disciplines plays a pivotal role in orchestrating a comprehensive response to the outbreak.

At the forefront of containment protocols lies surveillance and early detection, constituting the cornerstone of effective management. Rigorous surveillance mechanisms, both passive and active, aid in the identification of potential outbreaks and facilitate prompt intervention. Furthermore, early detection not only enables timely containment but also minimises the risk of transmission to humans, thereby averting a potential public health crisis.

Moreover, the implementation of stringent biosecurity measures assumes paramount significance in curtailing the spread of avian influenza. This encompasses a spectrum of interventions, including the restriction of the movement of poultry, decontamination protocols, and the enforcement of strict hygiene practices within poultry farms and live bird markets. Concurrently, the augmentation of biosecurity measures bolsters public confidence, safeguarding both public health and the economy.

In tandem with these efforts, the delineation of containment zones assumes a cardinal role in localised management. By delineating specific geographic areas and implementing stringent movement restrictions within these zones, the potential dissemination of the virus can be curtailed, thus preventing widespread transmission.

Furthermore, a robust communication strategy is indispensable in underpinning the success of containment protocols. Clear, transparent, and expeditious dissemination of information to the populace augments awareness, fosters compliance with control measures, and always unwarranted concerns. Communication forms the bedrock of public cooperation and adherence to containment measures, thereby serving as a linchpin in the overall containment strategy.

Concomitantly, the collaboration between public health authorities, veterinary agencies, and international organisations assumes pivotal importance. The synergy engendered by these collaborations not only amplifies the efficacy of containment efforts but also facilitates the exchange of best practices and resource mobilisation, thereby fortifying the global response to the outbreak.

However, it is imperative to underscore the indispensability of a robust contingency plan, characterised by dynamic, adaptive, and evidence-based strategies. The ever-evolving nature of avian influenza necessitates a proactive approach, characterised by continuous surveillance, periodic evaluation, and the recalibration of containment measures in consonance with emerging trends.

The Efficacy of containment protocols for avian influenza hinges upon the orchestration of a multifaceted, synergistic response that amalgamates the tenets of surveillance, biosecurity, communication, and collaboration. By fortifying these pillars, we not only fortify our defence against avian influenza but also underscore our commitment to safeguarding public health and global well-being.

Global Efforts in Controlling the Spread.

Avian influenza, also known as bird flu, has been a significant concern around the world due to its potential impact on both animal and human health. Two real-life stories related to avian influenza shed light on the importance of global cooperation and awareness in combating this infectious disease.

In 1997, a poultry outbreak of the H5N1 avian influenza virus in Hong Kong resulted in the culling of over 1.5 million chickens. This drastic measure was taken to prevent further transmission of the virus to humans. The incident raised awareness about the potential of avian influenza to jump from birds to humans and highlighted the need for proactive measures to prevent a possible pandemic.

Another significant event occurred in 2006 when cases of H5N1 avian influenza were reported in Turkey. This marked the first time the virus had been detected in humans outside of Asia. The rapid spread of the disease emphasised the importance of international cooperation in surveillance, reporting, and response to prevent the further spread of the virus across borders.

Global Efforts in Controlling the Spread of Avian Influenza: A Unified Front.

The battle against avian influenza has been a global endeavour, with nations and international organisations collaborating to stem the tide of this zoonotic threat. From the early outbreaks to the present day, these efforts have evolved, adapting to the challenges posed by the virus's changing dynamics.

Early Global Response:

The global response to avian influenza began in earnest in the late 20th century as outbreaks of various strains started to emerge. The World Health Organization (WHO), along with partners like the Food and Agriculture Organization (FAO) and the World Organisation for Animal Health (OIE), spearheaded initiatives to improve surveillance, strengthen veterinary services, and promote research into vaccines and treatments.

The turn of the century saw the highly pathogenic H5N1 strain spread across continents, prompting a more coordinated international response. Efforts focused on controlling the virus at its source—primarily in poultry—through culling, vaccination, and biosecurity measures. Public health campaigns aimed to reduce human exposure to infected birds, while research into antiviral drugs and vaccines intensified.

Recent Strategies:

In recent years, the global strategy has shifted towards a One Health approach, recognizing the interconnectedness of human, animal, and environmental health. This holistic strategy emphasises the need for cross-sectoral cooperation to address the ecological drivers of disease emergence and spread.

2020s and the Pandemic Preparedness:

The 2020s brought new challenges with the COVID-19 pandemic, which underscored the importance of pandemic preparedness. Building on lessons learned, global health authorities have emphasised the need for robust surveillance systems, rapid response capabilities, and equitable access to medical countermeasures.

2024 Efforts:

In 2024, the world will see a concerted effort to control avian influenza amidst other ongoing global health challenges. The CDC, in collaboration with the USDA and FDA, has been responding to a multistate outbreak of H5N1 in dairy cows and other animals in the United States, using a One Health approach. This includes enhanced surveillance, laboratory work to characterise the virus, and technical assistance for epidemiological studies. The UK has implemented policies to mitigate the impact of avian influenza in wild birds, focusing on surveillance and control within the remit of national law.

The global efforts to control the spread of avian influenza are a testament to the power of international collaboration. From early responses to the innovative strategies of 2024, the world has shown resilience and adaptability in the face of this ever-present viral threat. As we continue to navigate these challenges, the lessons learned will undoubtedly shape our approach to future outbreaks, ensuring a safer and healthier world for all.

Unveiling the Healing Arsenal: Treatment Options for Avian Influenza.

Picture this: a world where the viral storm retreats, where feathers and flesh find refuge from the invisible adversary. Our next topic, "Treatment Options," is the beacon of hope in this narrative. From antiviral drugs to cutting-edge research, we delve into the strategies that defy the virus's grip. Join us on this journey—a quest for healing, resilience, and a brighter avian horizon. The cure awaits; let's explore together.

Chapter 6.

Treatment Options.

Current Treatments for Avian Influenza.

Previously, we embarked on a comprehensive journey through the intricate web of containment and control strategies for avian influenza. We explored the global tapestry of efforts, from rigorous surveillance systems to international cooperation, all aimed at clipping the wings of this formidable viral adversary. We delved into the One Health approach, recognizing the interconnectedness of human, animal, and environmental health, and how this holistic strategy is pivotal in our ongoing battle against the avian influenza virus.

Now, we turn our focus to the beacon of hope in this narrative: treatment options. As we navigate through the possibilities, from antiviral medications to innovative therapies, we stand on the cusp of a new chapter in our fight against avian influenza. The quest for healing beckons us forward, promising new horizons in the management of this disease. Join us as we unravel the tapestry of treatment options, where science meets determination in the quest for a cure.

Avian influenza, commonly known as bird flu, is a viral infection that can cause illness in birds and humans. The disease has raised global concern due to its potential to cause severe illness and death in affected populations. Understanding the treatment options for avian influenza is crucial in managing and preventing its spread. In this article, we will explore various treatment approaches, including antiviral medications, supportive care, and vaccination, as well as the importance of early detection and prevention strategies. By gaining insights into the available treatment options, we can better equip ourselves to address the challenges posed by avian influenza and safeguard public health. Let's delve into the details and gain a comprehensive understanding of the treatment options for avian influenza.

Avian influenza, with its various strains such as H5N1 and H7N9, presents unique challenges due to its potential to cause severe respiratory illness and its ability to spread rapidly among bird populations. When it comes to treating avian influenza in humans, early detection and prompt initiation of appropriate treatment are integral in improving patient outcomes. Antiviral medications, such as oseltamivir (Tamiflu) and zanamivir (Relenza), are commonly recommended for the treatment of avian influenza. These medications work by inhibiting the replication of the influenza virus in the body, thereby reducing the severity and duration of the illness. It is essential for healthcare providers to promptly identify and initiate antiviral treatment in individuals suspected of avian influenza infection to minimise the risk of complications and transmission to others.

In addition to antiviral medications, supportive care plays a critical role in the treatment of avian influenza. Patients with severe cases may require hospitalisation and supportive interventions such as oxygen therapy, fluid management, and, in some cases, mechanical ventilation. Providing comprehensive supportive care is essential in managing the complications arising from avian influenza and improving patient survival rates. Moreover, vaccination against seasonal influenza and potential avian influenza strains is paramount in preventing infection and reducing the overall burden of the disease. Vaccination helps bolster the immune response and provides a layer of protection against avian influenza, especially for individuals at high risk of exposure, such as poultry workers and healthcare personnel.

Early detection and prevention are key components of effective avian influenza management. Surveillance and monitoring of avian populations, along with rapid identification of human cases, are crucial for implementing timely control measures. Public health initiatives aimed at educating the public about avian influenza, promoting good hygiene practices, and fostering collaboration between healthcare professionals, veterinarians, and policymakers are instrumental in minimising the impact of the disease. By enhancing awareness and preparedness, we can mitigate the potential threats posed by avian influenza and work towards ensuring the safety and well-being of communities worldwide.

Treatments for Avian Influenza in Birds.

Avian influenza, commonly known as bird flu, is a highly contagious viral disease that can affect birds and sometimes spread to humans. The treatment of avian influenza in birds is crucial in preventing the spread of the disease and minimising its impact on both bird populations and potential human health risks.

1. **Antiviral Medications:**
Antiviral medications such as oseltamivir and zanamivir are commonly used to treat avian influenza in birds. These medications are designed to inhibit the replication of the influenza virus, thereby reducing the severity and duration of the illness in infected birds. Proper administration of antiviral medications can help control outbreaks and limit the transmission of the virus within bird populations.

2. **Supportive Care:**

In addition to antiviral medications, providing supportive care to infected birds is essential for their recovery. Supportive care may include maintaining proper nutrition, hydration, and environmental conditions to improve the birds' immune response and overall well-being during the illness.

3. **Quarantine and Biosecurity Measures:**

Implementing strict quarantine and biosecurity measures in avian influenza-affected areas is critical to preventing further spread of the disease. By isolating infected birds and minimising contact with healthy flocks, the risk of transmission can be significantly reduced. Proper biosecurity protocols, including disinfection of equipment and restricted movement of birds, are essential components of controlling avian influenza outbreaks.

Treatments for Avian Influenza in Humans.

The emergence of avian influenza viruses with the potential to cause severe disease in humans has raised significant public health concerns. While prevention and control measures are paramount in limiting human exposure to avian influenza, the availability of effective treatments for infected individuals is essential in managing the disease and minimising its impact on human health.

1. **Antiviral Medications:**

Antiviral medications, particularly neuraminidase inhibitors such as oseltamivir and zanamivir, are considered the primary means of treating avian influenza in humans. Early initiation of antiviral treatment can reduce the severity of symptoms, shorten the duration of illness, and potentially lower the risk of complications in individuals infected with avian influenza viruses. Timely administration of antiviral therapy is critical for maximising its effectiveness in managing human cases of avian influenza.

2. **Supportive Care:**

Alongside antiviral medications, providing supportive care to individuals with avian influenza is essential for optimising their recovery and minimising the impact of the disease. Supportive care measures may include ensuring adequate hydration, monitoring for respiratory complications, and addressing any additional medical needs arising from the infection. In severe cases, supportive care in the form of respiratory support or intensive care may be necessary to manage complications associated with avian influenza.

3. **Vaccination and Immunization**:

While antiviral medications play a vital role in treating avian influenza in humans, vaccination and immunisation strategies also hold promise in mitigating the impact of the disease. Research into the development of vaccines that provide cross-protection against diverse avian influenza viruses is ongoing, to reduce enhancement of illness and enhance preparedness for potential pandemics. Vaccination efforts targeting high-risk populations, such as poultry workers and individuals with occupational exposure to birds, are important components of public health strategies aimed at preventing human cases of avian influenza.

The treatment of avian influenza in both birds and humans encompasses a multifaceted approach involving antiviral medications, supportive care, and comprehensive prevention measures. By addressing the unique challenges posed by avian influenza in each context, effective treatments can contribute to the control of the disease and the protection of both animal and human populations from its adverse effects.

Research and Development of New Antivirals.

From Containment to Cure: The Avian Influenza Challenge.

In our previous discussions, we navigated the complex landscape of avian influenza containment and control. We examined the global tapestry of efforts, from rigorous surveillance systems to international cooperation, all aimed at clipping the wings of this formidable viral adversary. From the bustling markets where live birds are sold to the meticulous hand washing rituals, we explored the strategies that safeguard both birds and humans.

Now, as we step into the realm of treatment, the horizon brightens. Research and development are our compass, guiding us toward new antiviral agents. The quest for effective medications—ones that can halt the virus's march—is relentless. We delve into the science, exploring polymerase inhibitors, attachment inhibitors, and the promise of combination therapies. The race to outwit the virus is on, and we're at the forefront.

Research and Development of New Antiviral:
In laboratories across the globe, scientists labour over molecules, seeking the Achilles' heel of avian influenza. T-705, a polymerase inhibitor, holds promise. DAS181, an attachment inhibitor, whispers of hope. The goal? To create agents that defy resistance, that bridge the gap between containment and cure. Combination therapies, like harmonious symphonies, may hold the key.

As we peer into the future, we see a mosaic of possibilities: vaccines, novel drugs, and universal solutions. The virus evolves, but so do we. The battle rages, but so does our determination. Join us on this journey—a quest for healing, resilience, and a brighter avian horizon. The cure awaits; let's explore together.

Advancements in Research and Development of New Antivirals for Avian Influenza

Avian influenza, commonly known as bird flu, is a highly contagious viral infection that affects birds and, in some cases, can be transmitted to humans. The continual threat posed by avian influenza has prompted significant research and development efforts by renowned research centres, aiming to identify effective antiviral treatments to combat the spread of this disease.

Research initiatives at esteemed institutions such as the Centers for Disease Control and Prevention (CDC) in the United States have been pivotal in advancing scientific knowledge and developing potential treatments for avian influenza. The CDC's research encompasses epidemiological studies, identification of treatment targets, and clinical trials to evaluate the efficacy of novel antiviral compounds.

Collaborating closely with global entities, the World Health Organization (WHO) has played a central role in coordinating international research efforts to combat avian influenza. By fostering partnerships with research institutions, public health agencies, and pharmaceutical companies, the WHO ensures the thorough evaluation of promising antiviral candidates for both safety and efficacy.

Moreover, academic research centres and pharmaceutical companies worldwide are actively engaged in multidisciplinary scientific endeavours to develop viable antiviral treatments for avian influenza. Researchers from diverse fields such as virology, immunology, pharmacology, and medicinal chemistry collaborate to explore innovative approaches to combat avian influenza.

Recent advancements in biotechnology and drug discovery have enabled the identification of novel molecular targets and the screening of vast chemical compound libraries for potential antiviral activity. Additionally, breakthroughs in structural biology and computer-aided drug design have facilitated the development of antiviral compounds with enhanced potency and specificity.

Despite these strides, developing new antiviral treatments for avian influenza is not without challenges. The virus's genetic diversity and ability to rapidly mutate necessitate a comprehensive and adaptable approach to drug development. Researchers are thus exploring novel strategies, including combination therapies, broad-spectrum antiviral agents, and immunomodulatory agents to counter the complexity of avian influenza and the host immune response to viral infection.

The research and development of new antiviral treatments for avian influenza represent a crucial area of scientific exploration with profound global health implications. Through collaborative efforts and leveraging cutting-edge scientific and technological advancements, researchers are making significant strides in advancing our understanding of avian influenza and identifying potential treatments. With continued dedication, it is anticipated that effective antiviral treatments for avian influenza will be developed, thereby mitigating the impact of this significant infectious disease.

Prepare to be captivated by the dynamic field of Public Health Policies!

Venture into the esteemed domain of **Public Health Policies**, where strategic frameworks are not merely regulatory measures but are transformative forces that fortify and elevate the health of populations. We stand at the threshold of introducing pioneering policies that are set to revolutionise the public health paradigm. These policies, stemming from meticulous research and inventive health initiatives, are ready to catalyse a worldwide health revival. The sense of expectation is tangible, and with equal enthusiasm, I await the opportunity to disclose the influential impact of these novel policies. Anticipate an enlightening exploration into the essence of public health, where each policy is crafted to instigate substantial improvements across the globe.

Chapter 7.

Public Health Policies.

National and International Policies for Pandemic Prevention

In our last engaging dialogue, we delved into the dynamic world of Research and Development for New Antivirals, a frontier where science meets innovation in the quest to outsmart avian influenza. We uncovered the promising avenues of polymerase inhibitors and attachment blockers and the potential of combination therapies to offer a robust shield against the virus's cunning tactics.

Now, we pivot to a broader canvas: National and International Policies for Pandemic Prevention. This is where governance meets science, where policies shape the global health landscape. As countries unite under the banner of health for all, we'll explore how recent amendments to the

International Health Regulations and the push for a global pandemic agreement are setting the stage for a safer, more resilient world. Join us as we dissect these policies, their impact, and the collective journey toward a future fortified against pandemics.

What is a public health policy?
Public health policy encompasses the decisions and actions taken by governments and health organisations to safeguard and enhance the well-being of a population. In the context of avian influenza in both birds and humans, public health policy plays a vital role in the prevention and control of the disease. This involves a range of measures such as surveillance, biosecurity in poultry farms, public awareness campaigns, and the development and implementation of vaccination programs. International cooperation is also essential in addressing avian influenza due to its transboundary nature. Through evidence-based policies and collaborative efforts, governments and health organisations

work to protect both animal and human populations from the threat of avian influenza.

National and International Policies for Pandemic Prevention.

When addressing the topic of national and international policies for the prevention of avian influenza, it is vital to underscore the critical role of proactive measures in safeguarding public health on a global scale. The world has witnessed the devastating impact of avian influenza outbreaks, underscoring the necessity of robust policies to prevent and mitigate the effects of such occurrences. This essay aims to explore the significance of national and international policies for avian influenza prevention, focusing on various strategies and approaches that can be implemented to effectively address this pressing issue.

At the national level, countries are tasked with developing and implementing comprehensive policies tailored to their specific healthcare infrastructure, population demographics, and socio-economic factors. An essential component of national policies for avian influenza prevention is the establishment of early warning systems to detect potential outbreaks. This involves investing in surveillance and monitoring mechanisms to track avian influenza and identify any emerging threats. Furthermore, countries should prioritise the development of robust healthcare systems with the capacity to respond swiftly and effectively to public health emergencies, including ensuring an adequate supply of essential medical resources such as vaccines, antiviral medications, and personal protective equipment, as well as bolstering healthcare workforce preparedness.

In addition to these measures, national policies for avian influenza prevention should emphasise the importance of public health education and awareness. By promoting hygiene practices, avian influenza vaccination programs, and responsible health behaviour, countries can empower their citizens to actively contribute to disease prevention efforts. Moreover, the implementation of quarantine protocols, travel restrictions, and border control measures can play a pivotal role in containing the spread of avian influenza within national borders.

Moving beyond national initiatives, the role of international cooperation and collaboration in avian influenza prevention cannot be overstated. Given the interconnected nature of our globalised world, avian influenza poses a transnational threat that necessitates cohesive and coordinated responses. International policies for avian influenza prevention should revolve around facilitating information sharing, resource mobilisation, and mutual assistance among nations. This can be achieved through platforms such as the World Health Organization (WHO) and other regional health agencies, which serve as key facilitators of communication and coordination during public health crises.

Furthermore, the development of global frameworks for avian influenza preparedness and response is crucial in establishing standardised protocols and best practices that can be adopted by countries worldwide. These frameworks can outline guidelines for data sharing, outbreak investigation, and the deployment of medical personnel and supplies to affected regions. Additionally, international policies should prioritise equitable access to avian influenza vaccines and medical treatments, ensuring that all countries, irrespective of their economic standing, have the means to protect their populations from potential avian influenza outbreaks.

The formulation and implementation of national and international policies for avian influenza prevention are integral to mitigating the impact of infectious disease outbreaks and safeguarding global public health. Through a combination of proactive measures at the national level and concerted international cooperation, it is possible to enhance our collective resilience against avian influenza. By prioritising early detection, robust healthcare infrastructure, public awareness, and global solidarity, policymakers can help build a future where the devastating impact of avian influenza is significantly reduced.

National and International Policies for Avian Influenza Pandemic Prevention:

A Global Commitment.

The flutter of wings, the distant call of migratory birds—these seemingly ordinary moments hold within them the potential for a silent storm: avian influenza. As the world grapples with the ever-present threat of zoonotic diseases, national and international policies emerge as our collective shield against pandemics. In this discourse, we unravel the intricate tapestry of avian influenza prevention strategies, weaving together science, governance, and global cooperation.

The Avian Menace.

Avian influenza, commonly known as bird flu, dances on the delicate edge between feathered flocks and human vulnerability. Its origins trace back centuries, but its impact reverberates through time. The virus, primarily harboured by wild birds, occasionally leaps species barriers, infecting domestic poultry and, rarely, humans. The consequences can be dire: economic losses, public health crises, and ecological imbalances.

National Policies:
A Mosaic of Preparedness.

1. Surveillance and Early Detection.

National policies lay the groundwork for vigilance. Robust surveillance systems, akin to watchful sentinels, scan the skies for signs of trouble. Governments invest in monitoring wild bird populations, tracking migratory routes, and identifying high-risk areas. The goal? To detect avian influenza outbreaks at their inception, before they spiral into pandemics.

2. **Biosecurity Measures.**

Imagine a poultry farm—a bustling ecosystem where birds thrive. Here, national policies mandate stringent biosecurity measures. Access control, disinfection protocols, and restricted movement zones become the norm. Farmers, veterinarians, and poultry workers receive training on disease prevention. The objective? To create an impermeable fortress against the virus.

3. **Contingency Plans.**

National policies are not mere documents; they are blueprints for action. Governments draft contingency plans, anticipating worst-case scenarios. These plans outline response mechanisms: culling infected flocks, implementing movement restrictions, and activating emergency funds. The message is clear: preparedness saves lives.

**International Cooperation:
A Symphony of Unity.**

1. The One Health Approach.
The avian influenza virus knows no borders. It flits across continents, carried by migratory birds. Hence, international policies embrace the One Health approach—a harmonious symphony where human, animal, and environmental health converge. United Nations agencies, the World Health Organization (WHO), and the Food and Agriculture Organization (FAO) join hands. Together, they compose a global score, emphasising collaboration, data sharing, and joint research.

2. The International Health Regulations (IHR).
Imagine a global treaty—a pact among nations to safeguard humanity. The International Health Regulations (IHR) serve this purpose. These regulations bind countries to report outbreaks promptly, share information transparently and coordinate responses. The IHR transforms

national policies into a global chorus, ensuring that no outbreak goes unnoticed.

3. **Pandemic Preparedness Agreements.**
The year 2024 witnessed a pivotal moment: the push for a global pandemic agreement. Countries convened, diplomats negotiated, and commitments were made. The agreement aims to streamline responses, allocate resources, and prevent chaos during pandemics. It's a testament to our shared vulnerability and collective resolve.

Research and Development: The Beacon of Hope.
As national and international policies set the stage, research and development illuminate the path forward. Scientists labour in laboratories, seeking antiviral agents, vaccines, and novel therapies. Polymerase inhibitors, attachment blockers, and combination treatments emerge. The virus evolves, but so do we. The race to outwit the avian influenza virus is relentless, fueled by the promise of healing.

The skies remain vigilant—the wild birds continue their ancient migrations. But beneath their wings, a global commitment unfolds. National policies fortify our borders, international cooperation bridges divide, and research kindles hope. Avian influenza may test our resilience, but our policies and collective efforts form an unyielding shield. As we navigate this avian odyssey, let us remember: that prevention is our anthem, unity is our strength, and science is our guiding star.

The Role of Health Organizations in Disease Control.

From Vigilance to Victory: The Role of Health Organizations in Disease Control.

In our recent voyage, we unfurled the global tapestry of pandemic prevention policies—national and international threads woven together to shield humanity. We explored surveillance systems, biosecurity measures, and the harmonious symphony of the One Health approach. These policies, like sentinels, stand guard against invisible foes, ensuring our well-being.

Now, let's pivot to the heart of the matter: **The Role of Health Organizations in Disease Control** . Imagine a web where the World Health Organization (WHO), the Centers for Disease Control and Prevention (CDC), and countless others collaborate. They're the architects of health resilience, orchestrating responses, disseminating knowledge, and fortifying our defences. Together, they decode outbreaks, track pathogens, and advise nations. Their mission? To transform chaos into clarity, and fear into facts.

, and hope.

Our forthcoming discourse will address the **Socio-Economic Impact of Avian Influenza**, scrutinising the profound implications on both economic stability and social welfare. We shall consider the disruption to the poultry industry, consequential unemployment, and the strain on healthcare systems. Additionally, we will assess the broader economic repercussions, including diminished agricultural productivity and the perturbation of international trade dynamics. This analysis aims to elucidate the intricate interplay between an avian influenza pandemic and socio-economic structures, thereby fostering a comprehensive understanding of its extensive and multifaceted effects.

Chapter 8

The Socio-Economic Impact.

The Socio-Economic Impact The Socio-Economic Impact of Avian Influenza.

Avian influenza, commonly known as bird flu, is a highly contagious viral disease that affects a wide range of birds, including chickens, turkeys, quails, and wild birds. In recent years, there has been growing concern about the spread of avian influenza and its potential impact on both the poultry industry and human health. Research has shown that avian influenza can have significant socio-economic implications, affecting not only the poultry farming sector but also the broader economy and public health systems.

From a research standpoint, numerous studies have highlighted the far-reaching consequences of avian influenza outbreaks. One key area of concern is the economic impact on poultry farmers and the wider agricultural industry. When an outbreak occurs, infected birds must be culled to prevent the spread of the disease. This can result in substantial financial losses for farmers, as they not only lose their existing stock but also face restrictions on movement and trade that can last for months. Furthermore, the costs associated with implementing biosecurity measures and disinfection protocols add further financial strain.

In addition to the direct impact on poultry farmers, avian influenza outbreaks can have ripple effects throughout the supply chain. Reduced consumer confidence in poultry products can lead to decreased demand, causing prices to plummet and creating additional hardships for producers. Moreover, restrictions on the movement of birds and poultry products can disrupt trade both domestically and internationally, leading to trade imbalances and market uncertainties.

Beyond the agricultural sector, avian influenza can also have profound socio-economic consequences at the societal level. Outbreaks of the disease can lead to job losses in rural communities that depend on poultry farming as a primary source of income. Moreover, the broader economy can be affected as reduced consumer spending and trade disruptions impact related industries such as transportation, retail, and food services.

From a public health perspective, avian influenza poses a significant risk to human health. While the virus primarily affects birds, there is a potential for it to mutate and spread to humans, leading to severe illness and even death. This not only poses a direct threat to human health but also places a considerable burden on healthcare systems, particularly in areas where resources may already be limited.

The socio-economic impact of avian influenza is multifaceted and far-reaching. From the agricultural sector to the broader economy and public health, the consequences of outbreaks can be severe. As such, proactive measures such as effective biosecurity protocols, rapid response plans, and international collaboration are essential in mitigating the impact of avian influenza and safeguarding both animal and human well-being.

The Shadow Pandemic: Avian Influenza's Economic Contagion.

As dawn breaks over the countryside, a farmer's routine is shattered by the discovery of lifeless poultry—victims of avian influenza. This scene, replicated across continents, is the harbinger of a shadow pandemic that transcends the boundaries of health and plunges deep into the economic veins of society.

The Economic Toll: A Global Affliction.

Avian influenza, or bird flu, is not merely a disease of birds; it's an economic malaise that infects industries, markets, and livelihoods. The World Bank warns of a potential global cost reaching a staggering $1.4 trillion in the first year of a pandemic[1]. The poultry industry, a linchpin of agriculture worldwide, faces the brunt of culling measures and market disruptions. In Ghana, the economic losses due to avian influenza have soared to $26.3 million, with poultry products plummeting by up to 25% in market value.

But the virus does not stop at the farm gate. It ripples through the economy, affecting trade, tourism, and even international relations. Simulation results predict a global export price increase of 9.63% in the event of simultaneous outbreaks[5]. This is not just a crisis of health; it's a crisis of economic stability.

Quantifying Costs: The Herculean Task.
To quantify the costs of avian influenza is to wrestle with a hydra—each head representing direct expenses, lost productivity, and long-term impacts on public health infrastructure. The World Bank's forecast paints a grim picture: a pandemic could cost up to 0.4% of GDP for middle and low-income countries. These

numbers, however, only scratch the surface of the true economic burden.

2024: A Year of Resilience and Recovery.

LIn 2024, the world stands vigilant against avian influenza. Efforts to quantify and mitigate the economic and social costs are more robust than ever, with health organisations and governments working in lockstep to develop effective prevention and response strategies.

A Call to Arms.

The economic toll of avian influenza is a clarion call for global action. It demands a concerted effort from all sectors—governments, health organisations, farmers, and consumers—to prevent, prepare for, and respond to outbreaks. As we face this challenge, let us remember that the true cost of avian influenza transcends numbers; it touches lives, livelihoods, and the very fabric of our global community.

Next Steps: Building Resilience.

As we continue our exploration, our next topic will delve into the role of health organisations in disease control. These institutions stand as pillars of resilience, guiding us through the storm of avian influenza with expertise and compassion. Join us as we uncover the strategies and efforts that shape our collective defence against this and future pandemics. Together, we can build a world more prepared, more responsive, and ultimately, more resilient.

The Socio-Economic Impact of Avian Influenza.

Avian influenza, also known as bird flu, has had a significant impact on societies and economies worldwide. The spread of avian influenza has caused untold devastation, affecting not only the health of individuals but also the economic stability of entire regions. In this article, we will delve into the socio-economic impact of avian influenza and explore its far-reaching consequences.

The economic impact of avian influenza is profound, with effects felt by individuals, businesses, and governments. The outbreak of avian influenza can result in substantial economic losses for the poultry industry, both in terms of production and trade. The culling of infected birds and the implementation of control measures can lead to a decrease in poultry production, causing financial strain for poultry farmers and related businesses. Moreover, trade restrictions imposed by other countries can further exacerbate the economic burden, limiting market access for poultry products and disrupting supply chains.

Beyond the poultry industry, avian influenza can also have a ripple effect on related sectors, such as transportation, tourism, and hospitality. The perception of a region being affected by avian influenza can deter tourists and investors, leading to a decline in tourism revenue and foreign direct investment. Additionally, the transportation of goods and people may be impacted, disrupting trade and travel activities and leading to economic downturns in affected areas.

The socio-economic impact of avian influenza extends to individual livelihoods, particularly those of vulnerable populations. In developing countries where poultry farming is a significant source of income and nutrition, the outbreak of avian influenza can have dire consequences for small-scale farmers and their families. Loss of livelihoods, decreased access to food, and limited healthcare resources can further exacerbate the socio-economic challenges faced by affected communities.

In addition to the economic repercussions, the spread of avian influenza can also strain public healthcare systems and resources. The emergence of avian influenza outbreaks places a burden on healthcare facilities, requiring additional resources and personnel to manage the surge in patients. Moreover, the potential for human-to-human transmission of avian influenza poses a public health risk, necessitating preparedness measures and investments in healthcare infrastructure to mitigate the impact on human health.

In response to the socio-economic impact of avian influenza, governments, international organisations, and stakeholders have implemented various measures to mitigate the effects and prevent future outbreaks. These measures include surveillance and early detection systems, vaccination programs for poultry, public awareness campaigns, and capacity-building initiatives to enhance healthcare systems' resilience.

Furthermore, research and development efforts have focused on the development of improved diagnostic tools, vaccines, and antiviral medications to combat avian influenza and reduce its impact on both animal and human health. International collaboration and information sharing have also played a crucial role in fostering a coordinated response to avian influenza, recognizing the interconnected nature of the global poultry industry and public health.

The socio-economic impact of avian influenza is profound, affecting livelihoods, economies, and public health systems. The widespread consequences of avian influenza underscore the importance of continued vigilance, preparedness, and collaborative efforts to mitigate its impact and prevent future outbreaks. By addressing the socio-economic challenges posed by avian influenza, societies and economies can strive to build resilience and safeguard the well-being of communities worldwide.

Chapter 9.

Future Outlook.

Innovations in Disease Surveillance and Management.

The future outlook of avian influenza, also known as bird flu, holds significant importance in the field of public health and veterinary science. As we look ahead, it is crucial to examine the potential trajectory of avian influenza and the measures that can be taken to mitigate its impact on both avian and human populations.

Avian influenza is caused by influenza A viruses that primarily infect birds. However, certain strains of avian influenza have demonstrated the ability to infect humans, giving rise to concerns about the potential for a global pandemic. Understanding the future outlook of avian influenza requires a multifaceted approach that encompasses virology, epidemiology, animal husbandry, and public health preparedness.

One of the key factors influencing the future trajectory of avian influenza is the continuous evolution of influenza viruses. The ability of these viruses to undergo genetic reassortment and mutation poses a perpetual challenge in predicting which strains may emerge as significant threats to human health. As avian influenza viruses continue to evolve, it is essential to monitor their genetic characteristics and assess their potential for human-to-human transmission.

In addition to virological considerations, the future outlook of avian influenza is also shaped by global agriculture and trade practices. The intensification of poultry production and the expansion of international poultry trade networks have contributed to the geographical spread of avian influenza viruses. Furthermore, the proximity of humans to domestic and wild bird populations increases the risk of viral spillover and transmission.

To address the future outlook of avian influenza, proactive measures must be implemented at the intersection of animal and human health. This includes the development of robust surveillance systems to monitor avian influenza in both avian and human populations. Early detection of novel influenza strains in birds is critical for initiating timely response measures to prevent potential outbreaks in humans.

Furthermore, research efforts focused on developing effective vaccines and antiviral treatments for avian influenza are essential components of preparedness. By investing in research and development, we can enhance our capacity to respond to emerging avian influenza threats and safeguard public health.

Another vital aspect of shaping the future outlook of avian influenza involves enhancing biosecurity measures in poultry farming and live bird markets. Implementing stringent biosecurity protocols can help reduce the risk of viral transmission between birds and minimise the potential for viral amplification within poultry populations.

In the broader context of public health preparedness, promoting awareness and education regarding avian influenza is paramount. Educating individuals about the risks associated with avian influenza exposure and the importance of practising personal hygiene and proper food handling can contribute to mitigating the potential impact of avian influenza on human health.

Considering the interconnected nature of global health security, international collaboration and information-sharing mechanisms are crucial for addressing the future outlook of avian influenza. By fostering partnerships and exchange of expertise among nations, we can collectively strengthen our ability to detect, respond to, and control avian influenza threats on a global scale.

The future outlook of avian influenza necessitates a comprehensive and collaborative approach that encompasses scientific research, surveillance, preparedness, and public health education. As we anticipate the evolving landscape of avian influenza, it is imperative to remain vigilant and proactive in our efforts to prevent and control potential outbreaks. By investing in scientific advancement, bolstering biosecurity measures, and fostering international cooperation, we can strive to mitigate the impact of avian influenza on both animal and human populations.

Innovations in Disease Surveillance and Management:
Harnessing Technological Advances to Combat Avian Influenza

Executive Summary:
To effectively combat the threat of avian influenza, we suggest that management embraces technological innovations in disease surveillance and management. This article explores cutting-edge advancements in data analytics, artificial intelligence, and digital

platforms, demonstrating their potential to enhance the detection, response, and control of avian influenza outbreaks.

Introduction:
Avian influenza poses a significant threat to global health, food security, and economies. The rapid spread of outbreaks necessitates innovative approaches to disease surveillance and management. Technological advancements offer unprecedented opportunities to strengthen our defences against this viral disease.

Data Analytics:
Data analytics plays a critical role in identifying patterns and trends, enabling proactive measures to prevent outbreaks. Advanced statistical models and machine learning algorithms can:
- Analyse vast datasets from various sources
- Detect anomalies and predict outbreak risk
- Identify high-risk areas and populations

Artificial Intelligence:
AI-powered systems can enhance surveillance and response by:
- Automating data analysis and reporting
- Providing real-time insights and alerts
- Supporting decision-making with predictive modelling

Digital Platforms:
Digital platforms can facilitate collaboration, data sharing, and communication among stakeholders, enabling:
- Real-time information exchange
- Coordinated response efforts
- Enhanced situational awareness

Implementation and Future Directions:
To fully leverage these innovations, we recommend:
- Investing in data infrastructure and analytics capabilities
- Developing AI-powered surveillance systems
- Establishing digital platforms for global collaboration.

Innovations in disease surveillance and management offer unprecedented opportunities to combat avian influenza. By embracing technological advancements, we can enhance global preparedness, response, and control. We urge management to harness these innovations, fostering a coordinated and effective approach to mitigate the threat of avian influenza.

Preparing for Future Health Crises.

Proactive Measures to Mitigate the Impact of Avian Influenza.

Executive Summary:

We suggest that healthcare authorities and governments adopt a proactive approach to prepare for future health crises, such as avian influenza outbreaks. This article outlines essential measures to enhance preparedness, including surveillance, vaccine development, public awareness, and global collaboration.

Avian influenza poses a significant threat to global health, with the potential to cause widespread illness and death. Proactive planning and preparedness are crucial to mitigating the impact of future outbreaks.

Surveillance and Detection:

Enhance surveillance capabilities to detect avian influenza outbreaks promptly, enabling swift response and control measures. This includes:
- Implementing robust monitoring systems
- Conducting regular testing and sampling
- Enhancing laboratory capacity

Vaccine Development and Distribution:

Develop and distribute effective vaccines to high-risk groups, such as poultry workers and healthcare professionals. This includes:
- Investing in research and development
- Establishing vaccine stockpiles
- Ensuring equitable distribution

Public Awareness and Education:

Educate the public on avian influenza risks, prevention strategies, and response measures. This includes:
- Launching awareness campaigns
- Providing accurate information
- Promoting community engagement

Global Collaboration and Coordination:

Foster global collaboration to share knowledge, resources, and best practices. This includes:
- Establishing international partnerships
- Sharing data and research findings
- Coordinating response efforts

Preparedness and Response Planning:

Develop and regularly update preparedness and response plans, including:
- Identifying high-risk areas and populations
- Establishing emergency response protocols
- Conducting regular drills and exercises

Preparing for future health crises requires proactive measures to mitigate the impact of avian influenza. By enhancing surveillance, vaccine development, public awareness, and global collaboration, we can reduce the risk of widespread illness and death. We urge healthcare authorities and governments to adopt a proactive approach, ensuring a coordinated and effective response to future outbreaks.

Chapter 10

Conclusion.

Integrating Lessons for Better Pandemic Preparedness: A Synthesis.

In conclusion, the comprehensive study on avian influenza has provided valuable insights into the global health concern posed by the virus. From understanding its biology and historical outbreaks to identifying symptoms, prevention strategies, containment, treatment options, public health policies, socio-economic impact, and future outlook, the research emphasises the importance of collaboration, innovation, and proactive measures in addressing and managing the threat of avian influenza. This knowledge will be pivotal in shaping effective strategies and policies for the prevention and control of avian

influenza to safeguard both human and animal
health.

Integrating Lessons for Better Pandemic Preparedness

The global community has faced numerous avian influenza outbreaks, each offering valuable lessons for enhanced preparedness. This synthesis integrates key takeaways from past experiences, forging a comprehensive framework for confronting the future of avian influenza.

The 1997 Hong Kong outbreak highlighted the importance of rapid detection and response, leading to the implementation of robust surveillance systems. The 2003 H7N7 outbreak in the Netherlands emphasised the need for effective biosecurity measures, while the 2004 H5N1 outbreak in Southeast Asia demonstrated the importance of coordinated global responses.

The 2013 H7N9 outbreak in China underscored the significance of:

- Enhanced poultry vaccination strategies
- Improved human-animal health interface surveillance
- Strengthened public health infrastructure and preparedness

Future avian influenza preparedness must be prioritised:

- Advanced genomics and sequencing technologies for early detection
- Innovative vaccine development and distribution strategies
- Integrated One Health approaches, unifying human, animal, and environmental health
- Regular simulation exercises and drills for crisis preparedness
- Strengthened global partnerships and multilateral agreements

The future of avian influenza preparedness also depends on addressing the following key areas:

- Enhancing biosecurity measures in poultry farms and live bird markets
- Improving public awareness and education on avian influenza risks and prevention
- Developing and deploying effective antiviral treatments and therapies
- Strengthening global surveillance and reporting systems
- Conducting regular risk assessments and vulnerability mapping

Furthermore, innovative technologies such as:

- Artificial intelligence and machine learning for predictive analytics
- Big data and genomics for early detection and tracking
- Digital platforms for real-time surveillance and response

Must be leveraged to enhance preparedness and response capabilities.

In conclusion, integrating lessons from past avian influenza outbreaks and prioritising a proactive, One Health approach will be crucial in mitigating the impact of future outbreaks. By fostering global collaboration, advancing scientific research, and leveraging innovative technologies, we can create a safer and more resilient world for all.

Let us look at each of the points mentioned earlier.

Enhancing biosecurity measures in poultry farms and live bird markets:

Effective biosecurity is crucial to preventing the spread of avian influenza in poultry. This includes measures such as strict hygiene practices, proper disposal of waste, and limiting human contact with birds. Implementing and enforcing robust biosecurity protocols in farms and markets can significantly reduce the risk of outbreaks and transmission.

Improving public awareness and education on avian influenza risks and prevention:

Raising public awareness and understanding of avian influenza is vital for preventing the spread of the disease. Educating the public on risks, symptoms, and prevention strategies can encourage responsible behaviour, such as reporting sick birds and practising good hygiene. Awareness campaigns and public outreach programs can play a key role in promoting a culture of prevention and preparedness.

Developing and deploying effective antiviral treatments and therapies:
Antiviral treatments and therapies are critical for managing avian influenza outbreaks. Research and development of effective treatments, such as vaccines and medications, can help reduce the severity and duration of outbreaks. Ensuring access to these treatments, particularly in high-risk areas, is essential for saving lives and preventing further transmission.

Strengthening global surveillance and reporting systems:
Global surveillance and reporting systems are essential for detecting and responding to avian influenza outbreaks. Enhancing these systems enables rapid sharing of information, coordinated responses, and targeted interventions. Strengthening surveillance capacities, particularly in high-risk areas, can

help prevent the spread of the disease and protect global health security.

Conducting regular risk assessments and vulnerability mapping:

Regular risk assessments and vulnerability mapping help identify areas most at risk of avian influenza outbreaks. These exercises enable targeted interventions, resource allocation, and preparedness measures. By identifying vulnerabilities and assessing risks, we can proactively mitigate the impact of potential outbreaks and protect public health.

Leveraging innovative technologies:

Innovative technologies, such as artificial intelligence, big data, and digital platforms, can revolutionise avian influenza preparedness and response. These technologies enable rapid detection, tracking, and prediction of outbreaks, facilitating targeted interventions and real-time response. Leveraging these technologies can significantly enhance global preparedness and save lives.

Prevention: A Global Imperative.

Enhancing biosecurity measures:
Biosecurity is the first line of defence against avian influenza. Implementing strict hygiene practices, proper disposal of waste, and limiting human contact with birds, poultry farms, and bird markets can significantly reduce the risk of outbreaks and transmission. This includes measures such as cleaning and disinfecting facilities, implementing quarantine protocols, and ensuring that workers wear personal protective equipment.

Effective biosecurity requires regular monitoring and enforcement and must be prioritised to prevent the spread of avian influenza. Farms and markets must work together to implement biosecurity protocols, share best practices, and conduct regular audits to ensure compliance. Moreover, governments and international organisations must provide support and resources to enhance biosecurity capacities, particularly in high-risk areas.

Improving public awareness and education:
Public awareness and education are critical components of avian influenza prevention and control. By understanding the risks and symptoms of avian influenza, individuals can take responsible actions to prevent transmission, such as reporting sick birds and practising good hygiene. Public awareness campaigns and education programs can promote a culture of prevention and preparedness, encouraging individuals to take proactive steps to protect themselves and their communities.

Education programs must target farmers, market workers, and the general public, and must be tailored to local languages and contexts. Moreover, public awareness campaigns must be sustained and repeated regularly to ensure that the message reaches a wide audience and is not forgotten over time. Governments, international organisations, and civil society must work together to promote public awareness and education, and to ensure that communities are empowered to prevent the spread of avian influenza.

Developing and deploying effective antiviral treatments and therapies:

Antiviral treatments and therapies are essential for managing avian influenza outbreaks. Vaccines and medications can help reduce the severity and duration of outbreaks, saving lives and preventing further transmission. Research and development of effective treatments are critical, as is ensuring access to these treatments, particularly in high-risk areas.

Vaccines must be developed and deployed quickly in response to outbreaks and must be effective against multiple strains of avian influenza. Medications must be made available and accessible, particularly in remote and resource-poor areas. Moreover, treatment protocols must be developed and disseminated to healthcare workers and must be based on the latest scientific evidence. Governments, international organisations, and the private sector must work together to develop and deploy effective treatments and to ensure that they reach those who need them most.

Strengthening global surveillance and reporting systems:

Global surveillance and reporting systems are the backbone of avian influenza prevention and control. By detecting and reporting outbreaks rapidly, countries can implement targeted interventions and prevent further transmission. Strengthening surveillance capacities, particularly in high-risk areas, is essential for global health security.

Surveillance systems must be robust, sensitive, and specific, and must be able to detect outbreaks quickly and accurately. Reporting systems must be rapid and reliable and must be linked to effective response mechanisms. Moreover, surveillance and reporting systems must be integrated with other health systems, such as human health and animal health systems, to ensure a coordinated response. Governments, international organisations, and civil society must work together to strengthen surveillance and reporting systems, and to ensure that they are sustainable and effective over the long term.

Conducting regular risk assessments and vulnerability mapping:

Regular risk assessments and vulnerability mapping are essential for identifying areas most at risk of avian influenza outbreaks. By identifying vulnerabilities and assessing risks, countries can prioritise targeted interventions and preparedness measures, reducing the impact of outbreaks.

Risk assessments must be based on the latest scientific evidence, and must take into account factors such as animal density, farm size, and market practices. Vulnerability mapping must identify areas with weak surveillance, poor biosecurity, and limited access to healthcare, and must prioritise interventions in these areas. Moreover, risk assessments and vulnerability mapping must be conducted regularly and must be updated to reflect changing circumstances and new information. Governments, international organisations, and civil society must work together to conduct regular risk assessments and vulnerability mapping, and to ensure that they are used to inform preparedness and response efforts.

Leveraging innovative technologies:
Innovative technologies offer game-changing solutions for avian influenza prevention and control. Artificial intelligence, big data, and digital platforms can enhance surveillance, detection, and response efforts, revolutionising global preparedness and response.

AI-powered algorithms can analyse vast amounts of data to detect early warning signs of outbreaks, while digital platforms can facilitate real-time reporting and information sharing. Big data analytics can identify patterns and trends in outbreak data, informing targeted interventions and preparedness measures. Moreover, innovative technologies can enhance collaboration and coordination among governments, international organisations, and civil society, facilitating a more effective and efficient response. Governments, international organisations, and the private sector must work together to leverage innovative technologies and to ensure that they are used to support global preparedness and response efforts.

Appendice.

Guidelines for Poultry Farmers:

A Practical Manual

Poultry farming is a significant contributor to the global food supply, providing a source of protein for millions of people worldwide. However, poultry farming also carries risks, including the potential for disease outbreaks and environmental pollution. To ensure the health and well-being of poultry, as well as the safety of the food supply, poultry farmers need to follow best practices and guidelines. This manual provides practical guidance for poultry farmers to ensure the health and well-being of their flocks, as well as the safety of the environment and the food supply.

I. Biosecurity
- Implement strict biosecurity measures to prevent the introduction and spread of diseases

- Ensure all personnel and visitors wear personal protective equipment (PPE) when entering the farm
- Sanitise all equipment and vehicles regularly
- Implement a robust vaccination program
- Monitor for signs of disease and report any suspicions to the relevant authorities immediately

II. Housing and Environment.
- Ensure housing is clean, dry, and well-ventilated
- Provide adequate space and enrichment for birds
- Implement a robust manure management system
- Ensure access to clean water and feed at all times
- Monitor temperature and humidity levels to ensure bird comfort

III. Nutrition and Feed.
- Provide a balanced and nutritious diet
- Ensure access to clean water at all times

- Monitor feed quality and report any concerns to the relevant authorities
- Implement a robust feed management system

IV. Health and Disease Management.

- Monitor bird health regularly
- Implement a robust disease management program
- Report any signs of disease to the relevant authorities immediately
- Ensure access to veterinary care at all times

V. Waste Management.

- Implement a robust waste management system
- Ensure all waste is disposed of in a sanitary and environmentally friendly manner
- Monitor waste management practices regularly

VI. Record Keeping.

- Keep accurate and detailed records of all farm activities
- Monitor and record bird health, feed consumption, and waste management practices

- Report any concerns or issues to the relevant authorities immediately.

Poultry farming carries significant responsibilities, including ensuring the health and well-being of birds, as well as the safety of the food supply and the environment. By following these guidelines, poultry farmers can help ensure the health and well-being of their flocks, as well as the safety of the food supply and the environment. Remember, biosecurity, housing and environment, nutrition and feed, health and disease management, waste management, and record-keeping are all critical components of responsible poultry farming practices.

Public Health Resources for Avian Influenza.

A Comprehensive Directory.

International Resources.

- **World Organisation for Animal Health (WOAH)**

Government Agencies.

- Centers for Disease Control and Prevention (CDC) - Avian Influenza (Flu)
- National Institutes of Health (NIH) - Avian Influenza Research

- United States Department of Agriculture (USDA) - Animal and Plant Health Inspection Service (APHIS)

Non-Governmental Organisations.

- World Animal Protection - Avian Influenza
- Global Alliance for Animals and People - Avian Influenza Programme
- International Association of Public Health Institutes (IANPHI) - Avian Influenza Resources

Academic and Research Institutions.

- University of California, Davis - Avian Influenza Research
- University of Minnesota - Center for Animal Health and Food Safety (CAHFS) - Avian Influenza
- Harvard T.H. Chan School of Public Health - Avian Influenza Research

Online Resources.

- PubMed - Avian Influenza Publications
- WHO Global Influenza Programme - Surveillance and Response
- CDC Avian Influenza (Flu) Website

Hotlines and Helplines.

- CDC Information Line: 1-800-CDC-INFO (232-4636)
- USDA APHIS Veterinary Services: 1-844-820-2234

Professional Associations.

- American Public Health Association (APHA) - Avian Influenza Resources
- American Veterinary Medical Association (AVMA) - Avian Influenza
- International Association of Avian Veterinarians (IAAV) - Avian Influenza Resources

Conferences and Workshops.

- World Health Organization (WHO) - Avian Influenza Meetings and Conferences
- International Conference on Avian Influenza
- American Public Health Association (APHA) Annual Meeting - Avian Influenza Sessions

Funding Opportunities.

- National Institutes of Health (NIH) - Avian Influenza Research Grants
- Centers for Disease Control and Prevention (CDC) - Avian Influenza Funding Opportunities
- World Health Organization (WHO) - Avian Influenza Research Grants.

This comprehensive directory provides a wide range of public health resources related to avian influenza, including international resources, government agencies, non-governmental organisations, academic and research institutions, online resources, hotlines and helplines, professional associations, conferences and workshops, and funding opportunities. These resources are essential for promoting and protecting public health, and for advancing research and response efforts related to avian influenza.

National Institutes of Health (NIH) - Avian Influenza Research Grants.

• Funding Opportunity Announcement (FOA) Title: "Avian Influenza Research and Development for Effective Treatments and Diagnostic Tools"

• Purpose: To support research on the avian influenza virus and its transmission, pathogenesis, and epidemiology, as well as the development of effective treatments and diagnostic tools.

• Eligibility: Domestic and foreign institutions, organisations, and businesses.

• Application Deadline: Varies.

Centres for Disease Control and Prevention (CDC) - Avian Influenza Funding Opportunities.

• Funding Opportunity Announcement (FOA) Title: "Avian Influenza Surveillance and Response"

• Purpose: To support surveillance, detection, and response to avian influenza outbreaks in the United States and globally.

• Eligibility: Domestic and foreign institutions, organisations, and businesses.

• Application Deadline: Varies.

World Health Organization (WHO) - Avian Influenza Research Grants

• Funding Opportunity Announcement (FOA) Title: "Avian Influenza Research and Development for Global Health Security"

• Purpose: To support research on the avian influenza virus and its transmission, pathogenesis, and epidemiology, as well as the development of effective treatments and diagnostic tools.

• Eligibility: Domestic and foreign institutions, organisations, and businesses.

• Application Deadline: Varies.

Conferences and Workshops.

- World Health Organization (WHO) - Avian Influenza Meetings and Conferences

  - Purpose: To bring together international experts to share knowledge, discuss challenges, and coordinate efforts on avian influenza surveillance, research, and response.

  - Frequency: Biennial.

- International Conference on Avian Influenza

- Purpose: To provide a platform for scientists, policymakers, and public health officials to share research findings, discuss policy issues, and coordinate responses to avian influenza outbreaks.
  - Frequency: Annual.
- American Public Health Association (APHA) Annual Meeting - Avian Influenza Sessions
  - Purpose: To provide a forum for public health professionals to share research findings, discuss policy issues, and coordinate responses to avian influenza outbreaks.
  - Frequency: Annual.

Training and Education.
- Centers for Disease Control and Prevention (CDC) - Avian Influenza Training and Education
  - Purpose: To provide training and education on avian influenza surveillance, detection, and response for public health professionals, laboratory personnel, and healthcare providers.
  - Format: Online courses, workshops, and conferences.

- World Health Organization (WHO) - Avian Influenza Training and Education

- Purpose: To provide training and education on avian influenza surveillance, detection, and response for public health professionals, laboratory personnel, and healthcare providers.

- Format: Online courses, workshops, and conferences.

- University of California, Davis - Avian Influenza Training and Education

- Purpose: To provide training and education on avian influenza research, surveillance, and response for graduate students, postdoctoral fellows, and public health professionals.

- Format: Online courses, workshops, and conferences.

Publications.

- Morbidity and Mortality Weekly Report (MMWR) - Avian Influenza Reports

- Purpose: To provide timely and accurate information on avian influenza outbreaks, surveillance, and response efforts.

- Frequency: Weekly.

- Emerging Infectious Diseases (EID) - Avian Influenza Articles

 - Purpose: To publish original research articles, reviews, and commentaries on avian influenza virus and its transmission, pathogenesis, and epidemiology.

 - Frequency: Monthly.

- Journal of Infectious Diseases (JID) - Avian Influenza Articles

 - Purpose: To publish original research articles, reviews, and commentaries on avian influenza virus and its transmission, pathogenesis, and epidemiology.

 - Frequency: Monthly.

Surveillance Systems.

- World Health Organization (WHO) - Global Influenza Surveillance and Response System (GISRS)

 - Purpose: To provide a global platform for sharing influenza surveillance data, detecting and responding to influenza outbreaks, and monitoring influenza virus evolution.

 - Frequency: Real-time.

- Centers for Disease Control and Prevention (CDC) - Influenza Division Surveillance and Response

   - Purpose: To provide surveillance data, detect and respond to influenza outbreaks, and monitor influenza virus evolution in the United States.

   - Frequency: Real-time.

- Food and Agriculture Organization of the United Nations (FAO) - Animal Influenza Surveillance and Response

   - Purpose: To provide surveillance data, detect and respond to animal influenza outbreaks, and monitor animal influenza virus evolution.

   - Frequency: Real-time.

Appendix of avian influenza from World Organisation for Animal Health (WOAH:

APPENDIX 2.3.4.1: BIOSAFETY GUIDELINES FOR HANDLING HIGHLY PATHOGENIC AVIAN INFLUENZA VIRUSES IN VETERINARY DIAGNOSTIC LABORATORIES
Introduction:
- The spread of highly pathogenic avian influenza (HPAI) viruses poses risks to humans, animals, and the environment.
- Handling HPAI viruses in veterinary diagnostic laboratories requires biosafety measures to prevent exposure and transmission.

A. Laboratory Design and Equipment.
- Designate a separate laboratory for handling HPAI viruses.
- Install safety cabinets, gloves, and face protection.
- Use sealed containers for transporting samples.

B. Personal Protective Equipment (PPE)
- Wear gloves, gowns, face shields, and respirators.
- Ensure proper fit and maintenance of PPE.

C. Sample Handling and Testing.
- Handle samples in a safety cabinet.
- Use appropriate disinfectants and sterilisation methods.
- Test samples using validated methods.

D. Decontamination and Disinfection.
- Use appropriate disinfectants and sterilisation methods.
- Decontaminate surfaces, equipment, and materials.

E. Waste Management.
- Dispose of waste according to local regulations.
- Autoclave or incinerate materials contaminated with HPAI viruses.

F. Training and Emergency Preparedness.
- Provide training on biosafety and emergency procedures.
- Establish an emergency response plan for accidents or spills.

G. Animal Handling and Care.
- Handle animals with appropriate PPE.
- Provide appropriate care and housing for animals.

H. Vaccination and Testing.
- Use appropriate vaccines and testing methods.
- Follow local regulations and guidelines.
- Decontaminate work surfaces and equipment with appropriate disinfectants effective against influenza viruses.
- All reusable PPE must be properly cleaned and decontaminated according to manufacturer's instructions after each use.
- Decontaminate all potentially infectious materials prior to disposal using an effective

method consistent with all local and state requirements.

- Materials that will be decontaminated outside the immediate laboratory should be placed in a durable, leak-proof container and closed for transport from the laboratory.

- Follow local, regional, state, national, and international regulations for waste disposal.

- State and local waste disposal regulations vary.

- Perform routine diagnostic specimen processing and testing in Biosafety Level 2 (BSL-2) laboratory facilities, adhering to standard precautions, safety equipment requirements, and facility specifications recommended for BSL-2.

- Manipulate diagnostic specimens in a certified Class II Biosafety Cabinet (BSC) or other containment devices, especially if there is a potential to generate aerosols (e.g., vortexing or pipetting).

- If you cannot perform a procedure within a BSC, use a combination of PPE and other containment devices (e.g., benchtop safety shield, centrifuge safety cups, or sealed rotor) designed to create a barrier between the specimen and the laboratory personnel.

Glossary.

Definitions of Key Terms Related to Avian Influenza.

Here are the definitions of key terms related to avian influenza:

Avian influenza: A type of influenza that affects birds, caused by the avian influenza virus.

Avian influenza virus (AIV): The virus that causes avian influenza, which can infect birds, humans, and other animals.

Subtype: A specific type of avian influenza virus, denoted by a combination of two numbers (e.g., H5N1, H7N9).

Hemagglutinin (H): A protein on the surface of the avian influenza virus that helps it attach to and enter host cells.

Neuraminidase (N): A protein on the surface of the avian influenza virus that helps it release from host cells.

Pandemic: A widespread outbreak of a disease that affects a large number of people across multiple countries or even continents.

Outbreak: A sudden increase in cases of a disease in a specific area or population.

Epidemic: A larger outbreak of a disease that affects a significant portion of a population or region.

Zoonotic: A disease that can be transmitted from animals to humans.

Transmission: The spread of a disease from one host to another.

Virulence: The severity of a disease caused by a virus.

Pathogenesis: The process by which a virus causes disease in a host.

Antigenic drift: A gradual change in the surface proteins of a virus over time, which can lead to reduced immune protection.

Antigenic shift: A sudden and significant change in the surface proteins of a virus, which can lead to a new subtype and reduced immune protection.

Vaccine: A preparation that stimulates the body's immune system to produce antibodies against a specific disease.

Vaccination: The administration of a vaccine to stimulate immunity against a disease.

Immunity: Protection against a disease conferred by the immune system.

Surveillance: The monitoring of disease trends and outbreaks to detect and respond to public health threats.

Isolation: The separation of infected individuals from others to prevent disease transmission.

Quarantine: The restriction of movement of individuals who have been exposed to a disease to prevent transmission.

Biosecurity: Measures taken to prevent the introduction and spread of diseases in animal populations.

Personal protective equipment (PPE): Gear worn to protect oneself from exposure to infectious agents.

Contact tracing: The identification and monitoring of individuals who have come into contact with someone infected with a disease.

Outbreak investigation: The systematic collection and analysis of data to identify the source and spread of a disease outbreak.

Influenza-like illness (ILI): A set of symptoms similar to those of influenza, including fever, cough, and sore throat.

Viral shedding: The release of virus particles from an infected individual into the environment.

Basic reproductive number (R0): A mathematical term that represents the average number of new cases generated by a single infected individual in a susceptible population.

Serial interval: The time between the onset of symptoms in a primary case and the onset of symptoms in a secondary case.

Attack rate: The proportion of individuals in a population who become ill during an outbreak.

Case fatality rate (CFR): The proportion of individuals who die from a disease among those who are infected.

Herd immunity: The protection of a population from an infectious disease when a sufficient percentage of individuals are immune.

Immune response: The body's natural defence against infection, which includes the production of antibodies and activation of immune cells.

Viral load: The amount of virus present in an individual's blood or other bodily fluids.

Shedding period: The time during which an infected individual is capable of transmitting the virus to others.

Incubation period: The time between exposure to a virus and the onset of symptoms.

Contagious period: The time during which an infected individual is capable of transmitting the virus to others.

Vector: An animal or insect that transmits a disease from one host to another.

Reservoir: The natural habitat or host of a disease-causing agent, where it can survive and multiply.

Zoonosis: A disease that can be transmitted from animals to humans.

One Health approach: A collaborative approach to address the interconnected health of humans, animals, and the environment.

Avian influenza outbreak: An occurrence of avian influenza in a specific geographic area or population.

Cluster: A group of cases of avian influenza that occur in close proximity to each other.

Index case: The first case of avian influenza identified in an outbreak.

Contact: An individual who has been in close proximity to an infected bird or person.

Transmission risk: The likelihood of avian influenza being transmitted from one host to another.

Environmental contamination: The presence of the avian influenza virus in the environment, such as in water or soil.

Animal health: The health status of animals in a given population or area.

Veterinary surveillance: The monitoring of animal health to detect and respond to disease outbreaks.

Avian influenza surveillance: The monitoring of bird populations to detect and respond to avian influenza outbreaks.

Sentinel surveillance: The use of sentinels (e.g., birds) to detect the presence of avian influenza in a population.

Active surveillance: The active search for cases of avian influenza in a population.

Passive surveillance: The reliance on reports of suspected cases of avian influenza from the public or healthcare providers.

Syndromic surveillance: The monitoring of symptoms and signs of illness to detect and respond to avian influenza outbreaks.

Outbreak response: The actions taken to control and contain an avian influenza outbreak.

Incident command system (ICS): A standardised management structure used to coordinate outbreak response efforts.

Personal protective equipment (PPE): Gear worn to protect oneself from exposure to infectious agents.

Infection control measures: Procedures put in place to prevent the spread of avian influenza, such as hand hygiene and cleaning and disinfection.

Contact tracing: The identification and monitoring of individuals who have come into contact with someone infected with avian influenza.

Quarantine: The restriction of movement of individuals who have been exposed to avian influenza to prevent transmission.

Culling: The killing of infected birds to prevent the spread of avian influenza.

Vaccination: The administration of a vaccine to prevent or reduce the severity of avian influenza infection.

Avian influenza vaccine: A vaccine specifically designed to protect against avian influenza.

Immunity: Protection against avian influenza conferred by the immune system.

Herd immunity: The protection of a population from avian influenza when a sufficient percentage of individuals are immune.

Zoonotic transmission: The transmission of avian influenza from birds to humans.

Human-to-human transmission: The transmission of avian influenza from one person to another.

Pandemic potential: The ability of avian influenza to cause a widespread outbreak across multiple countries or even continents.

Global health security: The protection of global health from infectious disease threats, including avian influenza.

International Health Regulations (IHR): A legal framework that aims to prevent and respond to public health threats, including avian influenza.

World Health Organization (WHO): A specialised agency of the United Nations responsible for international public health, including avian influenza.

Food and Agriculture Organization (FAO): A specialised agency of the United Nations responsible for food and agriculture, including animal health and avian influenza.

World Organisation for Animal Health (OIE): An international organisation responsible for animal health, including avian influenza.

National Institute of Allergy and Infectious Diseases (NIAID): A US research institute that conducts research on infectious diseases, including avian influenza.

Centres for Disease Control and Prevention (CDC): A US federal agency responsible for public health, including avian influenza.

European Centre for Disease Prevention and Control (ECDC): A European agency responsible for public health, including avian influenza.

Public health preparedness: The ability of public health systems to prepare for and respond to avian influenza outbreaks.

Emergency response plan: A plan that outlines the actions to be taken in response to an avian influenza outbreak.

Risk communication: The communication of risk information to the public during an avian influenza outbreak.

Crisis management: The management of an avian influenza outbreak as a crisis, including coordination and communication among stakeholders.